FRANKENSTEIN

Mary Shelley

AUTHORED by Jessica Montalvo
UPDATED AND REVISED by Aaron Suduiko

COVER DESIGN by Table XI Partners LLC
COVER PHOTO by Olivia Verma and © 2005 GradeSaver, LLC

BOOK DESIGN by Table XI Partners LLC

Published by GradeSaver LLC, www.gradesaver.com

First published in the United States of America by GradeSaver LLC. 2015

GRADESAVER, the GradeSaver logo and the phrase "Getting you the grade since 1999" are registered trademarks of GradeSaver, LLC

ISBN 978-1-60259-544-6

Printed in the United States of America

For other products and additional information please visit http://www.gradesaver.com

Table of Contents

Biography of Mary Shelley (1797–1851)

It was apparent that the life of Mary Wollstonecraft Godwin was going to be out of step with the ordinary from the moment of her birth on August 30, 1797. She had both unorthodox parents and an orthodox family structure: her father, William Godwin, was a celebrated philosopher and historian who had briefly been a Calvinist minister. A cold, remote man who overate grossly and borrowed money from anyone who would give him a loan, he had little time for anything but his philosophical endeavors. This intellectual single-mindedness was somewhat modulated by his passion for Mary Wollstonecraft. With the possible exception of William Blake, Wollstonecraft was the most influential of the Enlightenment radicals. Having declared herself independent at the age of twenty-one, she ran a school with her sisters and was the respected friend of the philosopher Samuel Johnson. While in France, she had an affair with an army captain, which ended in the birth of her first daughter, Fanny. After the soldier abandoned her and the child, she returned to England and attempted suicide. Happily or unhappily, she failed, and began writing in a variety of genres. It was her revolutionary feminist writings, however, that won her lasting fame.

The first meeting between Godwin and Wollstonecraft took place at a dinner party at Godwin's home. Drawn to each other by virtue of their shared philosophical beliefs, the two began an affair begun in the autumn of 1796. When Mary discovered that she was pregnant, the couple decided to marry in order to legitimate both of Mary's children. The couple, however, in adherence to their enlightened views, continued to live and work independently. The pair remained devoted to each other, and Godwin was devastated when Wollstonecraft died shortly after the birth of their daughter, Mary. Although he was fond of his daughters, the task of raising them alone proved too much for Godwin, and he immediately set about finding a second wife. His proposal to Maria Reveley, who would later become Mary's best friend, was rejected.

He later married Mary Jane Clairmont, the first woman to respond to his overtures. This second wife proved to be a cruel, shallow woman who neglected Fanny and Mary in favor of her own children. Mary (who was so lively that her father had nicknamed her Mercury) was frequently whipped for impertinence; rebellion came naturally to the headstrong Mary, and she refused to be subdued. Though the girls were given lessons in domesticity (cooking, cleaning, and other wifely duties) Mary could not feign interest in such pursuits: she would simply take up a book and let the dinner burn. Her father was the most important person in her life, and his favor meant everything to her. She excelled in her lessons and could hold her own in adult conversation often with the great minds of her time from a remarkably early age. Around the age of eight, she began reading the writings of her mother. By the time she was ten, she had memorized every word of them.

Mary spent hours at her mother's grave, reading or eating meals when the atmosphere at home was particularly bad. This habit continued well into her teens, when she was sent to live at Ramsgate with a Miss Petman. This move was prompted by Mary's frailty and inability to concentrate at home. From Ramsgate, she journeyed to Scotland to stay with Baxter, a close friend of her father's. Living with the Baxters was the happiest time that Mary had thereto known. When she returned to London a year later, she had grown into a woman. She became closer to her father than ever before, and the two engaged in constant philosophical debate. This served, predictably, to augment her stepmother's hatred.

The poet Percy Shelley, a devoted follower and friend of William Godwin's, began spending a great deal of time in the Godwin home. Although he was married, his presence made an immediate impression on Mary, who began to read poetry at his inducement. Shelley's genuine admiration for the works of Mary's mother earned him her trust she invited him to accompany her on her visits to her mother's grave, and the two became inseparable. Their intellectual kinship was passionately felt by both of them, and they rapidly fell in love. Godwin was furious at this development, and immediately barred the poet from his home. The couple, however, refused to be separated and began a clandestine correspondence. With the help of Mary's stepsister, they were able to elope.

Setting up housekeeping in London was expensive, and money was very tight for the newly married pair. Relations between them were somewhat strained: Shelley's first wife Harriet belatedly bore him a son, and his good friend Thomas Hogg became enamored of Mary. To make matters worse, Mary became pregnant; the child, a daughter, died shortly after birth. Mary fell into an acute depression.

Having conceived a dislike for London (perhaps as a result of their misfortunes), the couple began traveling: in the English countryside, in France, and elsewhere. Mary was writing profusely, and published *Frankenstein* in 1818. No one could have predicted the extent of the book's popularity: it would remain the most widely read English novel for three decades. Although it was maliciously rumored that Percy Shelley was the book's true author, Mary was catapulted to the forefront of the struggle for recognition then being waged by woman writers.

Tragically, Percy Shelley drowned in a shipwreck in 1822. Though Mary was devastated, she remained dedicated to her son, Percy Florence. She spent the remainder of her life championing her husband's neglected poetry, and was eventually successful in forcing its publication. Mary Wollstonecraft Shelley died in her sleep at age fifty-four.

Frankenstein Study Guide

The early nineteenth century was not a good time to be a female writer -- particularly if one was audacious enough to be a female novelist. Contemporary beliefs held that no one would be willing to read the work of a woman; the fantastic success of Mary Wollstonecraft Shelley's *Frankenstein* served to thoroughly disprove this theory.

Frankenstein established Shelley as a woman of letters when such a thing was believed to be a contradiction in terms; only the reputation of Madame de Stael surpassed Shelley's in Europe. De Stael, however, was more famous for continuing to publish her works despite the fact that the Emperor Napoleon had explicitly forbade her to do so, rather than for the quality of the works themselves.

Though *Frankenstein* is now customarily classified as a horror story (albeit the first and purest of its kind), it is interesting to note that Shelley's contemporaries regarded it as a serious novel of ideas. It served as an illustration of many of the tenets of William Godwin's philosophy, and did more to promote his ideas than his own work ever did. The novel does not, however, subscribe to all of Godwin's precepts. It stands in explicit opposition to the idea that man can achieve perfection -- in fact, it argues that any attempt to attain perfection will ultimately end in ruin.

Frankenstein is part of the Gothic movement in literature, a form that was only just becoming popular in England at the time of its publication. The Gothic mode was a reaction against the humanistic, rationalist literature of The Age of Reason; one might say it was ushered in by the death of Keats, the English author with whom Romanticism is perhaps most closely associated. *Frankenstein* might be seen as a compromise between the Gothic approach and the Romantic one: it addresses serious philosophical subjects in a fantastical manner. Though it confronts recognizable human problems, it can hardly be said to take place in a recognizably natural world. Some critics have suggested that this tension between Gothic and Romantic literary modes echoes the philosophical tension that existed between herself and her husband, the Romantic poet Percy Bysshe Shelley.

As the prejudice against women writers was quite strong, Shelley determined to publish the first edition anonymously. Despite this fact, the novel's unprecedented success paved the way for some of the most prominent women writers of the nineteenth century, including George Eliot, George Sand, and the Bronte sisters. All of them owed Mary a tremendous literary debt. Without the pioneering work of Mary Wollstonecraft Shelley, a great many female authors might never have taken up their pens; they might never have felt free to exhibit dark imagination, nor to engage in philosophical reflection. Without her, and the women whose work she made possible, English literature would be unquestionably the poorer.

Frankenstein Summary

Robert Walton, an English adventurer, undertakes an expedition to the North Pole. While on this expedition (which has been a lifelong dream of his), Walton corresponds with his sister by letter. Amid the ice floes, Walton and his crew find an extremely weary man traveling by dogsled. The man is near death, and they determine to take him aboard. Once the mysterious traveler has somewhat recovered from his weakness, Robert Walton begins to talk to him. The two strike up a friendship (Walton is very lonely and has long desired a close companion). The man is desolate, and for a long while will not talk about why he is traversing the Arctic alone. After becoming more comfortable with Walton, he decides to tell him his long-concealed story.

The speaker is Victor Frankenstein, for whom the book is named. He will be the narrator for the bulk of the novel. Born into a wealthy Swiss family, Victor enjoyed an idyllic, peaceful childhood. His parents were kind, marvelous people; they are presented as shining examples of the goodness of the human spirit. His father, Alphonse, fell in love with his wife, Caroline, when her father, a dear friend of his, passed away. Alphonse took the young orphan under his care, and as time passed they fell in love. He provides for his wife in grand style. Out of gratitude for her own good fortune, Caroline is extremely altruistic. She frequently visits the poor who live in her part of the Italian countryside. One day she chances upon the home of a family who has a beautiful foster daughter. Her name is Elizabeth Lavenza. Though they are kind, the poverty of Elizabeth's foster parents makes caring for her a financial burden. Caroline falls in love with the lovely girl on sight, and adopts her into the Frankenstein family. She is close in age to Victor, and becomes the central, most beloved part of his childhood. Elizabeth is Victor's most cherished companion. Their parents encourage the children to be close in every imaginable way Â as cousins, as brother and sister, and, in the future, as husband and wife.

Victor's childhood years pass with astonishing speed. Two more sons, William and Ernest, are born into the family. At this time, the elder Frankensteins decide to stop their constant traveling: the family finally settles in Geneva. Though Victor is something of a loner, he does have one dear friend: Henry Clerval, from whom he is inseparable. The two have utterly different ambitions: Victor has developed a passion for science, while Henry longs to study the history of human struggle and endeavor. Eventually, Victor's parents decide it is time for him to begin his university studies at Ingolstadt. Before his departure, Victor's mother passes away. On her deathbed, she tells Victor and Elizabeth that it is her greatest desire to see the two of them married. Victor leaves for university, still in mourning for his mother and troubled by this separation from his loved ones.

Meanwhile, in Geneva, life goes on. Because Caroline was so generous, Elizabeth learns to be gracious as well. When she is old enough to know her mind, she extends housing and love to a young girl named Justine, whose mother dislikes her and wishes to be rid of her. Though Justine is a servant in the Frankenstein household, Elizabeth, Ernest and William regard her as a sister.

At Ingolstadt, Victor's passion for science increases exponentially. He falls into the hands of Waldeman, a chemistry professor, who excites in him ambition and the desire to achieve fame and distinction in the field of natural philosophy. Thus begins the mania that will end in destroying Victor's life. Victor spends day and night in his laboratory. He develops a consuming interest in the life principle (that is, the force which imparts life to a human being). This interest develops into an unnatural obsession, and Victor undertakes to create a human being out of pieces of the dead. He haunts cemeteries and charnel houses. He tells no one of this work, and years pass without his visiting home. Finally, his work is completed: one night, the yellow eyes of the creature finally open to stare at Victor. When Victor beholds the monstrous form of his creation (who is of a gargantuan size and a grotesque ugliness), he is horror-stricken. He flees his laboratory and seeks solace in the night. When he returns to his rooms, the creature has disappeared.

Henry joins Victor at school, and the two begin to pursue the study of languages and poetry. Victor has no desire to ever return to the natural philosophy that once ruled his life. He feels ill whenever he thinks of the monster he created. Victor and Clerval spend every available moment together in study and play; two years pass.

Then, a letter from Elizabeth arrives, bearing tragic news. Victor's younger brother, William, has been murdered in the countryside near the Frankenstein estate. On his way back to Geneva, Victor is seized by an unnamable fear. Upon arriving at his village, he staggers through the countryside in the middle of a lightning storm, wracked with grief at the loss of his brother. Suddenly, he sees a figure, far too colossal to be that of a man, illuminated in a flash of lightning: he instantly recognizes it as his grotesque creation. At that moment, he realizes that the monster is his brother's murderer.

Upon speaking to his family the next morning, Victor learns that Justine (his family's trusted maidservant and friend) has been accused of William's murder. William was wearing an antique locket at the time of his death; this bauble was found in Justine's dress the morning after the murder. Victor knows she has been framed, but cannot bring himself to say so: his tale will be dismissed as the ranting of a madman. The family refuses to believe that Justine is guilty. Elizabeth, especially, is heartbroken at the wrongful imprisonment of her cherished friend. Though Elizabeth speaks eloquently of Justine's goodness at her trial, she is found guilty and condemned to death. Justine gracefully accepts her fate. In the aftermath of the double tragedy, the Frankenstein family remains in a state of stupefied grief.

While on a solitary hike in the mountains, Victor comes face to face with the creature, who proceeds to narrate what has became of him since he fled Victor's laboratory. After wandering great distances and suffering immense cold and hunger, the monster sought shelter in an abandoned hovel. His refuge adjoined the cottage of an exiled French family: by observing them, the monster acquired language, as well as an extensive knowledge of the ways of humanity. He was greatly aided in this by the reading of three books recovered from a satchel in the snow: Milton's *Paradise Lost*, Goethe's *Sorrows of Werter*, and a volume of *Plutarch's Lives*. The monster speaks with great eloquence and cultivation as a result of his limited but admirable education.

He developed a deep love for the noble (if impoverished) French family, and finally made an overture of friendship. Having already learned that his hideous appearance inspires fear and disgust, he spoke first to the family's elderly patriarch: this honorable old gentleman's blindness rendered him able to recognize the monster's sincerity and refinement (irrespective of his appearance). The other members of the family returned unexpectedly, however, and drove the creature from the cottage with stones.

The monster was full of sorrow, and cursed his creator and his own hideousness. He therefore determined to revenge himself upon Frankenstein, whose whereabouts he had discovered from the laboratory notebooks. Upon his arrival in Geneva, the creature encountered William, whose unspoiled boyish beauty greatly attracted him. The monster, longing for companionship, asked William to come away with him, in the hopes that the boy's youthful innocence would cause him to forgive the monster his ugliness. Instead, William struggled and called the monster a number of cruel names; upon learning that the boy was related to Victor, he strangled him in a vengeful fury. Drawn to the beauty of the locket, he took it, and fled to a nearby barn.

There, he found Justine, who had fallen into an exhausted sleep after searching all day and all night for William. The monster's heart was rent by her angelic loveliness, and he found himself full of longing for her. Suddenly, he was gripped by the agonizing realization that he would never know love. He tucked the locket into the folds of Justine's dress in an attempt to seek revenge on all withholding womankind.

The monster concludes his tale by denouncing Victor for his abandonment; he demands that Victor construct a female mate for him, so that he may no longer be so utterly alone. If Victor complies with this rather reasonable request, he promises to leave human society forever. Though he has a brief crisis of conscience, Victor agrees to the task in order to save his remaining loved ones.

He journeys to England with Clerval to learn new scientific techniques that will aid him in his hateful task. Once he has acquired the necessary data, he retreats to a dark corner of Scotland, promising to return to Henry when the job is done. Victor is nearly halfway through the work of creation when he is suddenly seized by fear. Apprehensive that the creature and his mistress will spawn yet more monsters, and thus destroy humanity, he tears the new woman to bits before the monster's very eyes. The creature emits a tortured scream. He leaves Victor with a single, most ominous promise: that he shall be with him on his wedding night.

Victor takes a small rowboat out into the center of a vast Scottish lake; there, he throws the new woman's tattered remains overboard. He falls into an exhausted sleep, and drifts for an entire day upon the open water. When he finally washes ashore, he is immediately seized and charged with murder. A bewildered Victor is taken into a dingy little room and shown the body of his beloved Henry, murdered at the creature's hands. This brings on a fever of delirium that lasts for months. His father comes to escort him home, and Victor is eventually cleared of all charges.

At home in Geneva, the family begins planning the marriage of Elizabeth and Victor. On their wedding night, Elizabeth is strangled to death in the conjugal bed. Upon hearing the news, Victor's father takes to his bed, where he promptly dies of grief.

Having lost everyone he has ever loved, Victor determines to spend the rest of his life pursuing the creature. This is precisely what the creature himself wants: now, Frankenstein will be as wretched and bereft as he is. For some time, the creator pursues his creation; he had chased him as far as the Arctic Circle when Walton rescued him. Though he cautions the sea captain against excessive ambition and curiosity, he contradictorily encourages the sailors to continue on their doomed voyage, though it will mean certain death. His reason: for glory, and for human knowledge. Finally, he is no longer able to struggle against his illness, and dies peacefully in his sleep. At the moment of his death, the creature appears: he mourns all that he has done, but maintains that he could not have done otherwise, given the magnitude of his suffering. He then flees, vowing that he will build for himself a funeral pyre and throw his despised form upon the flames.

Frankenstein Characters

Victor Frankenstein

He is the main character, a man driven by ambition and scientific curiosity. His quest for absolute knowledge and power will eventually end in his own ruin.

Elizabeth Lavenza

Victor's bride. Elizabeth is presented as being angelically good and incomparably beauty: she represents ideal womanhood and its promises of love and comfort.

Caroline

Victor's mother; a paradigm of motherly concern and generosity. Her death provides the catalyst for Victor's desire to transcend death. It is her last wish that Victor and Elizabeth be married.

Alphonse

Victor's father; yet another shining example of kindness and selflessness. His happiness depends on the happiness of his children. If they fail, he does as well; thus, their deaths prefigure his own.

William

The youngest son of the Frankenstein family. His death at the hands of the monster renders him a symbol of lost and violated innocence.

Henry Clerval

Victor's best friend since childhood. Fascinated with the history of mankind, he is Victor's intellectual opposite. He, too, will be murdered by the monster; he is perhaps a symbol of the destruction of Victor's own goodness and potential.

Justine

Though a servant in the Frankenstein household, she is more like a sister to Victor and Elizabeth. She is executed for William's murder, and thus becomes yet another martyr to lost virtue and innocence.

The Creature / The Monster

The work of Frankenstein's hands, the creature is his double, his persecutor, and his victim. The lives of him and his creator are inextricably entwined.

Robert Walton

The reader's representative in the novel, he is the person to whom Victor relates his story. He has much in common with Victor: ambition, drive, and the desire for glory.

De Lacey

The head of the household observed by the creature, de Lacey has been robbed of his fortunes as a result of his own kindness. His blindness makes him capable of recognizing the creature's sincerity and goodness despite his hideous appearance.

Felix

The son of de Lacey, he is devoted to his family and his mistress, Safie. Though noble, he drives the creature from the family cottage with stones. He thereby symbolizes one of the basic flaws in the human character: the hatred of difference.

Agatha

The daughter of De Lacey, she is an example of selfless womanhood, caring for her brother and her father despite their poverty and her own sadness.

Safie

The betrothed of Felix. She is presented as exotically beautiful, and is racially fetishized for her Turkishness. The de Lacey family wishes to marry her to Felix and convert her to Christianity.

Frankenstein Glossary

malignity

intense ill will; spite.

desolation

a state of complete emptiness or destruction.

gaolers

archaic spelling of 'jailers'.

despondency

a state characterized by lack of hope or courage.

inconsolable

unable to be comforted.

terrific

in the context of Shelley, 'terrifying'.

placid

peaceful; serene.

pertinacity

persistence.

natural philosophy

an antiquated branch of study, which encompassed a broad sense of studying how the world works. It maps most closely onto what we now call 'science', though other disciplines, such as math, were also included in this category.

charnel houses

houses for dead bodies.

physiology

in Shelley, the science of living things, and of life as a concept, in a broad sense.

indefatigable

persisting tirelessly.

peculiar

personal; particular.

science

a more general term in Shelley than it is today; it refers broadly to learning and knowledge.

imperious

urgent.

chimerical

imaginary; fanciful.

predilection

a bias in favor of something.

the philosopher's stone

an object sought by alchemists, believed to be able to turn any metal into silver or gold.

dissimilitude

diversity; dissimilarity.

syndic

chief magistrate.

Frankenstein Themes

Literary Reflexivity

The text of *Frankenstein* itself symbolizes many of the same themes that its contents symbolize. For example: Frankenstein's monster is a creature created by imbuing various old body parts with a new life; similarly, Shelley's texts include direct quotes and references to many older poems and literary works. The text therefore acts as a composite image of many older stories with "new life" breathed into them, just like the monster.

Creation

The text is virtually obsessed with creation events: Frankenstein creates the monster out of dead tissue; the monster conceives of himself by reading about the creation of Adam in *Paradise Lost*; the monster asks for Frankenstein to create a mate for him; what's more, three different levels of narrative are actually created: the letters that R. Walton sends his sister, telling of his time sailing to the North Pole; the story that Frankenstein tells Walton, embedded in the letters; and the story that Frankenstein's monster tells Frankenstein of his youth, embedded in Frankenstein's story. The text as a whole, in this way, can be seen as a continual exploration of what is means to create something.

Responsibility

One of the ways in which the text explores the creation event is by posing the question of what responsibility, if any, the creator bears to the created. Frankenstein shuns his monster almost immediately after creating him. The monster attributes blame to Frankenstein for this, and puts the onus on Frankenstein to right his wrongs by creating a mate for the monster. When Frankenstein refuses, the monster punishes him; Frankenstein ultimately comes to believe that it is his duty to kill the monster. The two feel bound to each other by the creation event, and it is this bond that, by the account of Frankenstein and the monster, establishes culpability on the part of the creator for the outcome of the created.

Causal Dependency

The structure of blame in the novel focuses on particular events that are supposed to have completely altered the trajectory of the future -- that is, events that were necessary for broad swaths of future events to have obtained. So, for example, Frankenstein doubts that he would have undertaken the creation of Frankenstein if his father had not scoffed at his son's interest in alchemy and the like (Volume I, Chapter 1). Similarly, the monster blames his creator's neglect and deformed craftsmanship for his own bad lot in life (Volume II, Chapter 7). The reader is thereby invited to question whether this is actually a fair appraisal of causal relation and responsibility.

Promethean Hubris

The alternative title of *Frankenstein* is *The Modern Prometheus*, and the story is true to this moniker: in Greek mythology, Prometheus stole fire from the gods and gave it to humanity; he was subsequently bound and punished eternally for his crimes. Similarly, Frankenstein discovered how to give life to things -- a power thought divine -- and is subsequently punished by the endless tragedy delivered unto him by his creation.

Isolation

Isolation manifests both macrocosmically and microcosmically in the novel. The framing narrative is set on a ship sailing to the North Pole, arguably the most isolated point on the globe; more microcosmically, Frankenstein isolates himself from the rest of society by creating life, thereby giving himself a unique status to which no one else can relate; his monster is more directly isolated, because he is the only one of his kind.

Natural Law

The novel poses a question of where the line is drawn between what we *can* do and what we *ought* to do. It is shown to be scientifically possible for Frankenstein to create a living being out of dead tissue; yet there is an odd sense of paradox here: though the act seems wholly unnatural, is it not the case that it *is* natural by virtue of the fact that it can be done? The notion of scientific progress might suggest that Frankenstein was right to create such a being and conduct this research out of interest in expanding humanity's knowledge and mastery over the world; yet the horrific consequences of the experiments suggest that he might be the case that he never should have gone down the path of creating life by himself. This moral puzzle is one of the main issues the novel invites the reader to explore.

Frankenstein Quotes and Analysis

*I felt the greatest eagerness to hear the promised narrative, partly from
curiosity, and partly from a strong desire to ameliorate his fate, if it were
in my power. I expressed these feelings in my answer.*

*"I thank you," he replied, "for your sympathy, but it is useless; my fate is
nearly fulfilled. I wait but for one event, and then I shall repose in peace.
I understand your feeling," continued he, perceiving that I wished to
interrupt him; "but you are mistaken, my friend, if thus you will allow me
to name you; nothing can alter my destiny listen to my history, and you
will perceive how irrevocably it is determined."*

Preface, Letter 6

In this passage, Frankenstein conveys to Walton the belief that the course of his life -
- his *fate* -- is bound to the monster he created. In this way, he has been enslaved by
his own creation because his one goal in life has become to destroy it.

*No human being could have passed a happier childhood than myself. My
parents were possessed by the very spirit of kindness and indulgence. We
felt that they were not the tyrants to rule our lot according to their
caprice, but the agents and creators of all the many delights which we
enjoyed. When I mingled with other families, I distinctly discerned how
peculiarly fortunate my lot was, and gratitude assisted the development of
filial love.*

Volume I, Chapter 2

What's interesting to note, which Frankenstein highlights here, is that he had a
childhood characterized by loving, caring, present parents. This contrasts directly
with Frankenstein's prompt abandonment of his monster, following its creation.

*Natural philosophy is the genius that has regulated my fate; I desire,
therefore, in this narration, to state those facts which led to my
predilection for that science. When I was thirteen years of age, we all
went on a party of pleasure to the baths near Thonon: the inclemency of
the weather obliged us to remain a day confined to the inn. In this house I
chanced to find a volume of the works of Cornelius Agrippa. I opened it
with apathy; the theory which he attempts to demonstrate, and the
wonderful facts which he relates, soon changed this feeling into
enthusiasm. A new light seemed to dawn upon my mind; and, bounding
with joy, I communicated my discovery to my father. My father looked*

carelessly at the title page of my book, and said, "Ah! Cornelius Agrippa!
My dear Victor, do not waste your time upon this; it is sad trash."

If, instead of this remark, my father had taken the pains to explain to me
that the principles of Agrippa had been entirely exploded, and that a
modern system of science had been introduced, which possessed much
greater powers than the ancient, because the powers of the latter were
chimerical, while those of the former were real and practical; under such
circumstances, I should certainly have thrown Agrippa aside, and have
contented my imagination, warmed as it was, by returning with greater
ardour to my former studies. It is even possible that the train of my ideas
would never have received the fatal impulse that led to my ruin. But the
cursory glance my father had taken of my volume by no means assured
me that he was acquainted with its contents; and I continued to read with
the greatest avidity.

Volume I, Chapter 2

Here, Victor claims that he never would have gone down the road that ultimately led
to the creation of the monster if his father had responded differently to his interest in
alchemy. In this way, one might say that Victor's father turned him 'into a monster',
just as Victor created a monster all his own.

"The ancient teachers of this science," said he, "promised impossibilities,
and performed nothing. The modern masters promise very little; they
know that metals cannot be transmuted, and that the elixir of life is a
chimera. But these philosophers, whose hands seem only made to dabble
in dirt, and their eyes to pore over the microscope or crucible, have
indeed performed miracles. They penetrate into the recesses of nature,
and show how she works in her hiding places. They ascend into the
heavens: they have discovered how the blood circulates, and the nature of
the air we breathe. They have acquired new and almost unlimited powers;
they can command the thunders of heaven, mimic the earthquake, and
even mock the invisible world with its own shadows."

Such were the professor's words--rather let me say such the words of fate,
enounced to destroy me. As he went on, I felt as if my soul were grappling
with a palpable enemy; one by one the various keys were touched which
formed the mechanism of my being: chord after chord was sounded, and
soon my mind was filled with one thought, one conception, one purpose.
So much has been done, exclaimed the soul of Frankenstein--more, far
more, will I achieve: treading in the steps already marked, I will pioneer
a new way, explore unknown powers, and unfold to the world the deepest
mysteries of creation.

Volume 1, Chapter 3

The reaction of Frankenstein's first professor to his interest in alchemy, similar to his father's reaction, only spurs him on in pursuit of the path that will ultimately lead to creating the monster. Note the language of fate: throughout the novel, Frankenstein describes the tragic events of his life as a course that was determined for him. He attributes little-to-no agency to himself.

> *Remember, I am not recording the vision of a madman. The sun does not more certainly shine in the heavens, than that which I now affirm is true. Some miracle might have produced it, yet the stages of the discovery were distinct and probable. After days and nights of incredible labour and fatigue, I succeeded in discovering the cause of generation and life; nay, more, I became myself capable of bestowing animation upon lifeless matter.*

Volume I, Chapter 4

Frankenstein's language prefacing the creation of his monster underscores the text's preoccupation with proof and verification: he is invested in convincing the reader that the events he describes are both true and scientifically tenable.

> *I see by your eagerness, and the wonder and hope which your eyes express, my friend, that you expect to be informed of the secret with which I am acquainted; that cannot be: listen patiently until the end of my story, and you will easily perceive why I am reserved upon that subject. I will not lead you on, unguarded and ardent as I then was, to your destruction and infallible misery. Learn from me, if not by my precepts, at least by my example, how dangerous is the acquirement of knowledge, and how much happier that man is who believes his native town to be the world, than he who aspires to become greater than his nature will allow.*

Volume I, Chapter 4

The reserved nature which Frankenstein has about conveying the actual mechanism by which he created the monster does two things: it establishes a degree of narrative unreliability because we know that he is intentionally withholding information from Walton; it is also somewhat ironic that he is withholding the scientific mechanism, given his preoccupation with substantiating the claims of his story.

> *But I forget that I am moralising in the most interesting part of my tale; and your looks remind me to proceed.*

Volume I, Chapter 4

This brief comment after Frankenstein digresses on the context within which he created his monster is rather telling of the narrative as an overall piece: part of the game in *Frankenstein* is for the reader to absorb the events and decide on the moral implications for herself.

I started from my sleep with horror; a cold dew covered my forehead, my teeth chattered, and every limb became convulsed: when, by the dim and yellow light of the moon, as it forced its way through the window shutters, I beheld the wretch -- the miserable monster whom I had created. He held up the curtain of the bed; and his eyes, if eyes they may be called, were fixed on me. His jaws opened, and he muttered some inarticulate sounds, while a grin wrinkled his cheeks. He might have spoken, but I did not hear; one hand was stretched out, seemingly to detain me, but I escaped, and rushed down stairs. I took refuge in the courtyard belonging to the house which I inhabited; where I remained during the rest of the night, walking up and down in the greatest agitation, listening attentively, catching and fearing each sound as if it were to announce the approach of the demoniacal corpse to which I had so miserably given life.

Volume 1, Chapter 5

Note that in the one brief moment shared between the creator and the created before Frankenstein flees, the monster smiles at him. This lends credibility to the argument that Frankenstein was prejudiced against the monster from his very inception, and spurned him where he might otherwise have raised him to be a reasonably well-adjusted being.

"I can hardly describe to you the effect of these books. They produced in me an infinity of new images and feelings that sometimes raised me to ecstasy, but more frequently sunk me into the lowest dejection."

Volume II, Chapter 7

The monster says this in describing the three books with which he learned how to read -- *Paradise Lost, Plutarch's Lives,* and *Sorrows of Werter*. It relates the monster to both the novel as a whole, and to Frankenstein: Frankenstein also formulated much of his identity from books in his youth; and the whole as a home is largely structured by allusions and excerpts from other, earlier texts.

"You, who call Frankenstein your friend, seem to have a knowledge of my crimes and his misfortunes. But in the detail which he gave you of them he could not sum up the hours and months of misery which I endured, wasting in impotent passions. For while I destroyed his hopes, I did not satisfy my own desires. They were for ever ardent and craving; still I desired love and fellowship, and I was still spurned. Was there no injustice in this? Am I to be thought the only criminal when all human kind sinned against me? Why do you not hate Felix who drove his friend from his door with contumely? Why do you not execrate the rustic who sought to destroy the saviour of his child? Nay, these are virtuous and immaculate beings! I, the miserable and the abandoned, am an abortion, to be spurned at, and kicked, and trampled on. Even now my blood boils at the recollection of this injustice.

"But it is true that I am a wretch. I have murdered the lovely and the helpless; I have strangled the innocent as they slept, and grasped to death his throat who never injured me or any other living thing. I have devoted my creator, the select specimen of all that is worthy of love and admiration among men, to misery; I have pursued him even to that irremediable ruin. There he lies, white and cold in death. You hate me; but your abhorrence cannot equal that with which I regard myself. I look on the hands which executed the deed; I think on the heart in which the imagination of it was conceived, and long for the moment when these hands will meet my eyes, when that imagination will haunt my thoughts no more."

Volume III, Chapter 7

This is part of the monster's final monologue to Walton, after Frankenstein has died on the ship. Note that the monster has not actually found any sense of justice in spite of taking revenge: the only one who could make him happy was Frankenstein, by making him a mate -- something that he refused to do. He also agrees to what Frankenstein has said all along: because of his actions, he is 'a wretch'. However, it is important to note that he thinks he is a wretch because of the actions he took in seeking revenge against Frankenstein. So, it seems that he only *became* a wretch in *response* to Frankenstein rejecting him and calling him a wretch -- making it something of a self-fulfilling prophecy.

Frankenstein Letters 1-4 Summary and Analysis

Letters 1-4:

We are introduced to Robert Walton, a 28-year-old sea captain who is embarking on a journey to the North Pole region in order to find a passage from the Pacific to the Atlantic. He writes the letters to his sister, Mrs. Saville, in London, England. He has talked about making this expedition for six years: it has been a favorite dream of his, and he is pleased that he finally has a chance to make good on his promise to himself. Other dreams, such as becoming a poet or a playwright, have not worked out. Therefore, this vision must succeed. The writer of letters is thrilled that he will satisfy an "ardent curiosity" by setting foot on a part of the world never visited by man. As he prepares for voyage by taking practice trips in the North Sea of Russia, he is worried that he has no friend on the trip who will be able to sustain his disappointment should the dream not work out. He admits this is a romantic, emotional need, but it is there. Unfortunately he does not connect at all with the other men, even though he is very fond of his lieutenant and the ship's master. He is nevertheless extremely excited for his journey.

Once actually on the voyage, things are going well. But a strange thing happens. In the middle of the ocean, on sheets of ice, they spy a sleigh pulled by dogs with a large figure driving. He disappears, leaving the entire crew in puzzled wonderment. The next day, another sleigh is at the side of the ship, on the brink of destruction amidst the ice. This time, however, there is a regular-sized human there, asking to where the ship is bound. He boards the ship, nearly frozen and completely fatigued. When he is a bit recovered, Walton asks what he is doing up here. The stranger says he was tracking someone who fled from him. Apparently, it was the large figure Walton and his men saw earlier. Walton begins to spend time with the stranger. He is morosely unhappy, and when Walton talks about how he might be sacrificing his life on this expedition for the sake of knowledge, the stranger breaks down and decides to tell him the tale he has kept secret in order to reverse that opinion.

Analysis:

The structure of the book is arranged: we know that the unnamed stranger will be the general narrator, and Walton, substituting for all readers, will be the audience to whom he speaks. Shelley is setting up a number of themes in this clever kind of introduction. Walton's intense desire for discovery and the unknown, to the point that he would risk his life at sea, molds him along the lines of the epic hero type. Diction such as "glorious" and "magnificent" is used to describe his mission. Walton is consumed by the need to be immortal by doing what has never been done previously. He suffers from hubris and believes that he is invincible, destined to complete this dangerous journey. That this ultra-confident attitude upsets the stranger so much (he likens Walton's curiosity to drinking from a poisonous cup) is telling. The stranger believes that the quest for new knowledge can lead to self-destruction. While the idea sounds strange, it is a key theme to remember.

Walton's undertaking of this journey is a comment upon the larger society as well as upon his character: it is the outside world that is constantly urging its members to leap tall boundaries, that they might gain recognition and fame. Walton's values are definitely questionable. It does not seem that he really belongs on this mission, with so little experience, but he refuses to let this dream go. He is highly motivated and in his prime, a younger version of the weathered stranger, who had the same ideals at one point but has had to relinquish them. That Walton complains of not having peers to whom he can relate illustrates the most basic human need of companionship. Anything with an iota of humanness feels such a compulsion for friendship and emotional ties; anybody would be justified in going great lengths to find these things.

Frankenstein Chapters 1-4 Summary and Analysis

Chapter 1:

Frankenstein begins his tale, sensibly enough, with his childhood: he is from a wealthy and well-respected Swiss family. His parents met, he tells us, when his father went in search of a dear old friend. This man, named Beaufort, had fallen into poverty and obscurity; when the elder Frankenstein finally found him, he was entirely wretched and very near death. His daughter, Caroline, attended him with almost-religious devotion. Upon Beaufort's death, Caroline turned to Master Frankenstein for comfort, and the pair returned to Geneva together; a few years later, they were married.

During the first years of their marriage, the Frankensteins traveled constantly, for the sake of Caroline's fragile health. They divided their time among Germany, Italy, and France; their first child, Victor, was born in Naples, Italy. Victor's parents adored him, and he adored them in turn; his childhood, from the very first, was wholly idyllic. Until he was five, Victor was an only child, and both he and his parents felt the absence of other children strongly.

Caroline Frankenstein made a habit of visiting the poor: since she herself had been saved from poverty, she felt it her duty to improve the lot of those who did not share her good fortune. One day, she discovered an angelic girl-child, with fair skin and golden hair, living with a penniless Italian family. As the girl was an orphan, and her adoptive family lacked the means to care for her, the Frankensteins determined to raise the child as their own. The child, whose name was Elizabeth Lavenza, became Victor's sister and his constant companion, as well as the object of his unquestioning worship. For him, she is his most beautiful, most valuable possession.

Analysis:

This chapter is primarily concerned with the theme of family and kinship. The absolute necessity of human contact and emotional ties is stressed here: the elder Frankenstein goes through great trouble to visit his impoverished friend, and Caroline, too, is selflessly concerned with the needs of others (her father, her family, and the poor). It is important to note that Beaufort's ruin is itself connected to his decision to cut himself off from his former friends and live in absolute isolation; it is his isolation, more than his poverty, which leads to his death.

Because Victor speaks in first person, the other characters are presented as they relate to him ("my father, my mother, my sister"). At the beginning of his narrative, Victor is deeply embedded within a traditional family structure, and we develop our first impressions of his character in relation to it. His childhood is almost implausibly ideal; the reader therefore expects Victor to reflect the love and beauty with which he was surrounded as a boy.

A number of the relationships described in this chapter are structured as a relation between a caretaker and a cared-for: that between Caroline's father and Caroline; Victor's father and Caroline; the Frankensteins and Elizabeth; and between Victor and Elizabeth, to name a few. In this way, Shelley suggests that human connection and, to state the case rather more plainly, love itself is dependent upon one's willingness to care for another person particularly if that other person is defenseless, or innocent, and thus unable to care for themselves. The elder Frankenstein takes Caroline in after she is left penniless and an orphan; similarly, the family takes in the orphaned Elizabeth Lavenza to save her from a life of bitter poverty. Shelley subtly argues that there is nothing more wretched than an orphan: one must care for one's children, since one is responsible for bringing them into the world. This idea will become extremely important with the introduction of the monster, in that Victor's refusal to care for his own creature will say a great deal about the morality of his experiment.

Chapter 2:

The family ceases to travel after the birth of their second son. They return home to Switzerland, to their estate at the foot of the Alps. Young Victor prefers not to surround himself with a great many casual friends; instead, he is very intimate with a select few. These include a brilliant boy named Henry Clerval, renowned for his flights of imagination, and, of course, his beloved Elizabeth. Though Victor says that there can be no happier childhood than his, he confesses that he had a violent temper as a child. His temper was not directed at other people, however: it manifested itself as a passionate desire to learn the secrets of heaven and earth. Clerval, by contrast, was fascinated by questions of morality, heroism, and virtue.

At Geneva, Elizabeth's "saintly soul" serves to soothe and temper Victor's burning passion for study. Without her, his interest in his work might have developed an obsessional quality.

Frankenstein is full of pleasure as he recounts these scenes from his childhood, since they remain untainted by his recent misfortune. He can, however, see how his early scholarly endeavors foreshadow his eventual ruin.

At the age of thirteen, he becomes fascinated with the work of Cornelius Agrippa (a Roman alchemist who attempted to turn tin into gold and men into lions). His father tells him that the book is pure trash; Victor does not heed him, however, since his father does not explain why the book is trash. The system of "science" that Agrippa propounds has long since been proven false; Victor, unaware of this, avidly reads all of Agrippa's works, as well as those of his contemporaries, Paracelsus and Albertus Magnus. Victor shares their desire to penetrate the secrets of nature, to search for the philosopher's stone and the elixir of life. The quest for the latter becomes his obsession. Though he acknowledges that such a discovery would bring one great wealth, what Victor really longs for is glory.

Victor is also preoccupied with the question of how one might communicate with or even raise the dead. He finds no answer in the works of his Roman idols, and becomes entirely disillusioned with them when he witnesses a lightning storm. Since the Romans have no satisfactory explanation for this phenomenon, Victor renounces them entirely and devotes himself (at least for the time being) to the study of mathematics. Destiny, however, will return him to the problems of natural philosophy.

Analysis:

The reader is gradually introduced to those aspects of Victor's character that will lead to his downfall. He tells us that he possesses "a thirst for knowledge."

The narrator begins to pick apart and identify the aspects of his personality that will eventually lead to his downfall. He possesses what he calls a "thirst for knowledge." Thirst, of course, is a fundamental human need, necessary to one's very survival. Victor's desire to learn, therefore, is driven by nothing so insubstantial as curiosity: it is instead the precondition of his very being. Shelley thereby indicates that there is a compulsive quality to Victor's scholarship: it is something very close to madness.

Elizabeth is positioned here, quite literally, as a "saint." It is her gentle, feminine influence that saves Victor from his obsession during his time at Geneva. The influence of women, and of femininity, is thus presented as offering hope of salvation it inspires one to temperance and kindness.

Though both Victor and Clerval have passionate and creative characters, they express them very differently. Henry does it openly, with songs and plays; Victor, by contrast, does it privately, amidst books and philosophical meditations. His reading is directed toward the learning of secrets of forbidden knowledge. This predisposition to secrecy plays an essential role in Victor's scientific work and its consequences.

The question of the place of chance and destiny in Victor's fate also arises in this chapter. Victor "chances" upon the volume of Cornelius Agrippa; he suggests that he would never have become so fascinated with the alchemists if only his father had explained why their work was worthless. He also says that "destiny" brought him back to the study of natural philosophy: in this way, Victor attempts to absolve himself of culpability for his later actions. The word "creation" is deployed for the first time here, in reference to natural philosophy: Victor refers to it as "abortive creation." The idea of both creation and abortion will become highly significant in later chapters.

Chapter 3:

When he is seventeen, Victor's family decides to send him to the university of Ingolstadt, so that he might become worldlier. Shortly before his departure, Elizabeth falls ill with scarlet fever. Caroline, driven almost mad by worry, tends to her constantly, with complete disregard for the risk of contagion. Though Elizabeth recovers thanks to her extraordinary care, Caroline herself contracts the fever. On her deathbed, she joins Elizabeth and Victor's hands and says that her happiness is dependent upon their eventual marriage. With that, she dies. Victor cannot quite believe that his beloved mother is gone; he is stricken with grief and delays his departure to Ingolstadt. Elizabeth, determined to at least partially fill the void left by Caroline's death, devotes herself to caring for the surviving family.

Clerval comes to visit Victor on his last evening at home. Though Clerval is desperate to accompany Victor to university, his prosaic merchant father will not allow him to do so. Victor is certain, however, that Clerval will not remain bound to the crushing dullness of his father's business.

Upon his departure from Geneva, Victor reflects on the fact that he knows no one at Ingolstadt; he has always been unable to enjoy the company of strangers. However, his spirits are lifted by the thought of acquiring new knowledge.

The first person he encounters at Ingolstadt is <u>Krempe,</u> a professor of natural philosophy. This meeting is described as the work of an evil influence the "Angel of Destruction." The professor is astounded at the absurd and outdated science that Victor has read in the past, and tells him to begin his studies completely anew. At first, the narrator is indifferent to the idea of returning to science: he has developed a deep contempt for natural philosophy and its uses. This changes, however, when Victor attends a lecture given by a professor named Waldman. Victor is completely enraptured by the ideas of Waldman, who believes that scientists can perform miracles, acquire unlimited powers, and "mock the invisible world with its own shadows." He decides to return to the study of natural philosophy at once; he visits Professor Waldman the following day to tell him that he has found a disciple in Victor Frankenstein.

Analysis:

Caroline's decision to nurse Elizabeth, even though it means losing her own life, serves to indicate both Caroline's own selflessness and the high value placed on self-sacrifice in the book as a whole. Caroline on her deathbed is described as being full of "fortitude and benignity"; the irreproachable manner in which she has lived her life means that she can die peacefully, certain of her eternal reward. In telling Victor and Elizabeth that her happiness was dependent upon their union, Caroline makes their marriage a consummate symbol of earthly order and joy. The centrality of this event to the novel's trajectory thus becomes clear.

Victor's departure from home is both a coming of age and a dark foreshadowing of things to come. There is nothing affirmative in his departure from home: it is immediately preceded by his mother's death, the journey itself is "long and fatiguing," and he knows no one at all at Ingolstadt. At university, the obsessive pursuit of knowledge will come to take the place of Victor's friends and family; it will both substitute for human connection and make any such connection impossible.

The epic rhetoric of Waldman's lecture is quite striking, in that he makes the scientist out to be a god:

"...[They] have performed miracles. They penetrate into the recesses of nature and show how she works in her hiding-places. They ascend into the heavens...They have acquired new and almost unlimited powers; they can command the thunders of heaven, mimic the earthquake, and even mock the invisible world with its own shadows."

That this rhetoric inflames Victor is telling: what seduces him back to the world of natural philosophy is the hope of becoming a god, free of earthly law and limitations. He has become mad with the desire for not only discovery, but also for omnipotence (the state of being all-powerful) and omniscience (the state of being all-knowing). Victor tells us that Waldman's words were the "words of fate"; it was at this moment that his destiny was decided. Here, again, Victor absolves himself of guilt and locates the source of his ruin squarely outside himself, outside the purview of his own will: the fault lies not with him, but with fate, or destiny.

It is not accidental that the reader now learns the narrator's last name Frankenstein for the first time. This serves to depersonalize him and to distance him from the reader, thus signifying the abyss of experimentation into which he will soon fall. Indeed, "Frankenstein" can be seen as a separate persona, the embodiment of the narrator's god/scientist self (as distinct from the culpable humanity represented by "Victor").

Chapter 4:

Waldman makes Victor his cherished protégé, and does a great deal to accelerate the course of his education. Natural philosophy and chemistry become Victor's sole occupations. Laboratory work particularly fascinates him, and he soon finds himself secluded there for days at a time. Victor's great skill and unusual ardor impress his professors and classmates alike. Two years pass in this manner; the lure of scientific pursuit is so great that Victor does not once visit his family at Geneva.

Victor develops a consuming interest in the structure of the human frame: he longs to determine what animates it, what constitutes the "principle of life." Seized by a "supernatural enthusiasm," he begins to explore life by studying its inevitable counterpart: death. He rapidly verses himself in the rudiments of anatomy, and begins pillaging graveyards for specimens to use in his dissections. Victor discovers the secret of how to generate life through a sudden epiphany. He does not, however, share the content of this revelation with Walton (and, by extension, with the reader), because his own knowledge resulted in misery and destruction.

Even immediately following his epiphany, Victor hesitates before using his newfound skill, as he must first fashion a body. He determines to make one of gigantic proportions, so as to make his work somewhat easier. Victor eagerly anticipates the day when "a new species would bless [him] as its creator and source, [and] many happy and excellent natures would owe their being to [him]." He is drunk with the magnitude of his own power, and reflects, "No father could claim the gratitude of his child so completely as [Frankenstein] should deserve [that of his creations]."

His midnight labors occur while Victor is in a trance-like state, and he pillages graveyards and tortures living creatures in the name of his unholy labors. His work completely possesses his soul, and the seasons pass without his taking note of them.

Though Victor briefly worries about his father, who has been anxiously awaiting a letter from his son for over a year, he deludes himself into believing that the elder Frankenstein would understand and approve of his endeavors. In retrospect, he realizes that the pursuit of knowledge should be serene: when it is overly passionate, it takes on the character of an obsession. Simple pleasures are thereby destroyed; study itself becomes a thing "not befitting the human mind."

Analysis:

The fact that two years pass without Victor's visiting his family speaks poorly for his character. Though he knows his father and Elizabeth long to see him, he remains completely absorbed in his work. This indicates that Victor's capacity for altruism and benevolence has been utterly destroyed by his obsession; it also suggests that his character itself is deeply flawed. There is something fundamentally selfish in Victor, and his scientific pursuits are themselves the product of a desire for gross self-aggrandizement: he wants to create men who will worship him as their god.

The themes of chance and fate arise once again in this chapter. Frankenstein is on the point of returning to Geneva "when an incident happens" to change his mind. This plot device in which an expectation is expressed, only to be dashed a moment later by a seemingly chance occurrence is a common one in the novel. It serves at least two narrative purposes. On the one hand, it fills the reader with alternating currents of hope and despair: while we long for Frankenstein to save himself, we realize that his ruin is inevitable. This inevitability is both narrative (in that the beginning of the book makes it clear that Frankenstein's destruction has already occurred) and character-based: that is, we see how the elements of Victor's personality can lead only to his own downfall. The plot device of dashed expectation also serves to suggest that the course of destiny is unalterable. One's fate is determined, and there is little or nothing that any of us can due to change it.

Though Victor hesitates before beginning his research and after discovering the principle of life, he scoffs at his own discretion, saying that "cowardice or carelessness" have delayed or prevented many remarkable discoveries. He harbors real contempt for prudence and caution, believing them to be nothing but limitations upon what Man's capabilities. Frankenstein believes that Man should attempt to reverse death, to alter divine handiwork. Clearly, Victor will have to be punished for his hubris for his disrespect of both natural and heavenly boundaries.

Frankenstein becomes progressively less human that is to say, more monstrous as he attempts to create a human being. He tortures living creatures, neglects his family, and haunts cemeteries and charnel houses. As his morals suffer, his health does as well: he becomes pale and emaciated. Frankenstein's work is literally sickening the man who was once called Victor.

Frankenstein Chapters 5-8 Summary and Analysis

Chapter 5:

On a chill night of November, Victor finally brings his creation to life. Upon the opening of the creature's "dull yellow eye," Victor feels violently ill, as though he has witnessed a great catastrophe. Though he had selected the creature's parts because he considered them beautiful, the finished man is hideous: he has thin black lips, inhuman eyes, and a sallow skin through which one can see the pulsing work of his muscles, arteries, and veins.

The beauty of Frankenstein's dream disappears, and the reality with which he is confronted fills him with horror and disgust. He rushes from the room and returns to his bedchamber. He cannot sleep, plagued as he is by a dream in which he embraces and kisses Elizabeth, only to have her turn to his mother's corpse in his arms.

He awakens late at night to find the creature at his bedside, gazing at him with a fond smile. Though the monster endeavors to speak to him, he leaps out of bed and rushes off into the night. He frantically paces the courtyard for the remainder of the night, and determines to take a restless walk the moment that morning comes.

While walking in town, Frankenstein sees his dear friend Henry Clerval alight from a carriage; overjoyed, he immediately forgets his own misfortunes. Clerval's father has at last permitted him to study at Ingolstadt; the two old friends shall therefore be permanently reunited. Henry tells Victor that his family is wracked with worry since they hear from him so rarely. He exclaims over Frankenstein's unhealthy appearance; Victor, however, refuses to discuss the details of his project.

Victor searches his rooms to make certain that the monster is indeed gone. The next morning, Henry finds him consumed with a hysterical fever. Victor remains bedridden for several months, under the assiduous care of Henry, who determines to conceal the magnitude of Victor's illness from his family. Once Victor can talk coherently, Henry requests that he write a letter, in his own handwriting, to his family at Geneva. There is a letter from Elizabeth that awaits his attention.

Analysis:

In this chapter, Victor's scientific obsession appears to be a kind of dream -- one that ends with the creature's birth. He awakens at the same moment that the creature awakens: the moment the creature's eyes open, Frankenstein's own eyes are opened to the horror of his project. He is wracked by a sickness of both mind and body; this reflects the unnatural character of his endeavor, in which he attempted to take the place of god.

The narrator's sentences become abbreviated, abrupt, indicating his nervous, paranoid state. It is significant that Victor dreams of his mother and Elizabeth: as women, they are both "naturally" capable of creation (through giving birth). With their deaths, the natural creation and earthly virtue they represent dies as well. Victor's kiss is the kiss of death, and his marriage to Elizabeth is represented as being equivalent to both a marriage to his mother and a marriage with death itself.

At the moment of his birth, the creature is entirely benevolent: he affectionately reaches out to Frankenstein, only to have the latter violently abandon him. Despite his frightful appearance, he is as innocent as a newborn child -- and, in a sense, this is precisely what he is. Victor's cruel treatment of the creature stands in stark contrast to both his parents' devotion and Clerval's selfless care: he renounces his child at the moment of its birth. The reader begins to recognize the profoundly unethical character of Frankenstein's experiment and of Frankenstein himself.

Chapter 6:

Elizabeth's letter expresses concern for Victor's well-being, and gratitude to Henry for his care. She relates local gossip and recent family events. The family's most trusted servant, Justine Moritz, has returned to the family after being forced to care for her estranged mother until the latter's death. Victor's younger brother, Ernest, is now sixteen years old and aspires to join the Foreign Service; his other brother, William, has turned five and is doing marvelously well. Elizabeth implores Victor to write, and to visit, as both she and his father miss him terribly. Frankenstein is seized by an attack of conscience and resolves to write to them immediately.

Within a fortnight (two weeks), Victor is able to leave his chamber. Henry, after observing his friend's distaste for his former laboratory, has procured a new apartment for him and removed all of his scientific instruments. Introducing Clerval to Ingolstadt's professors is pure torture, in that they unfailingly exclaim over Victor's scientific prowess. Victor, for his part, cannot bear the praise, and allows Henry to convince him to abandon science for the study of Oriental languages. These -- along with the glorious melancholy of poetry -- provide Frankenstein with a much-needed diversion.

Summer passes, and Victor determines to return to Geneva at the end of autumn. Much to his dismay, his departure is delayed until spring; he is, however, passing many marvelous hours in the company of Clerval. They embark on a two-week ramble through the countryside, and Victor reflects that Henry has the ability to call forth "the better feelings of his heart"; the two friends ardently love one another.

Slowly, Victor is returning to his old, carefree self. He takes great joy in the natural world, and is able to forget his former misery. The two are in high spirits upon their return to university.

Analysis:

With Elizabeth's letter, we realize how utterly Victor has been cut off from the outside world. His narration of his first two years at Ingolstadt mentions few proper names, and concerns itself not at all with anyone else. The reader realizes how much time has passed, and how much has changed in faraway reader. We learn the names of Victor's brothers, and of the existence of Justine. Elizabeth's relation to Justine is much like Caroline's relation to Elizabeth: she cares for the less fortunate girl and heaps praise upon her, calling her "gentle, clever, and extremely pretty."

Justine's history, however, illustrates two of the novel's darker themes: the inevitability of atoning for one's sins, on the one hand, and the kind of suffering that atonement entails, on the other. Justine's cruel mother could not bear her, and had her sent away; after Justine's departure, her cherished children died, one by one, and left her utterly alone. She therefore had to rely upon Justine to care for her on her deathbed. This amply illustrates the code of justice propounded by the novel: one must always pay for one's cruelty, and pay with the thing that one holds most dear.

Victor's abandonment of science and natural philosophy is illustrative of his irrational attempt to deny that the events of the past two years have ever occurred. Victor seems to truly believe that he is impervious to harm: he does not pursue his lost creature, but goes about his life at university with supreme carelessness. He takes up languages and poetry -- two things in which he has never before shown the slightest interest -- and attempts to forget all that has come before. Victor thus displays a highly questionable relationship to reality: unless directly confronted by his mistakes, he refuses to acknowledge that he has made them at all. He is exceedingly weak, as his prolonged illness (which was both mental and physical) makes clear.

Ending the chapter at the height of springtime, Shelley emphasizes Victor's wish to be reborn. The reader, however, already knows that such a wish is entirely in vain.

Chapter 7:

At Ingolstadt, Victor and Henry receive a letter from Victor's father: William, Victor's youngest brother, has been murdered. While on an evening walk with the family, the boy disappeared; he was found dead the following morning. On the day of the murder, Elizabeth had allowed the boy to wear an antique locket bearing Caroline's picture. Upon examining the corpse, Elizabeth finds the locket gone; she swoons at the thought that William was murdered for the bauble. She comes to blame herself for his death. Victor's father implores him to come home immediately, saying that his presence will help to soothe the ravaged household. Clerval expresses his deepest sympathies, and helps Victor to order the horses for his journey.

On the way to Geneva, Victor becomes seized by an irrational fear. Certain that further disaster awaits him at home, he lingers for a few days at Lausanne. Summoning all his courage, he sets out again. Victor is moved to tears at the site of his native city, since his estrangement from it has been so prolonged. Despite his joy at being reunited with Geneva, his fear returns. He arrives at night, in the midst of a severe thunderstorm. Suddenly, a flash of lightning illuminates a figure lurking among the skeletal trees; its gigantic stature betrays it as Frankenstein's prodigal creature. At the sight of the "demon," Victor becomes absolutely certain that he is William's murder: only a monster could take the life of so angelic a boy.

Victor longs to pursue the creature and warn his family of the danger he represents. He fears that he will be taken for a madman if he tells his fantastic story, however, and thus resolves to keep silent.

At the Frankenstein estate, Victor is greeted with a certain melancholy affection. His brother, Ernest, relates a piece of shocking news: Justine, the family's trusted maidservant, has been accused of William's murder. The missing locket was found on her person on the night of the murder. The family -- particularly Elizabeth -- passionately believes in her innocence, and avers that their suffering will only be magnified if Justine is punished for the crime. They all dread Justine's trial, which is scheduled to take place at eleven o'clock on the same day.

Analysis:

The account of William's death is written in highly disjointed language: the sentences are long, and frequently are interrupted by semicolons, as though each thought is spilling into another. This indicates the magnitude of the distress felt by the narrator's father as he writes. Letters, in general, play a central role in the novel: it begins and ends with a series of letters, and many important details of plot and character are related through them. They enable Shelley (who has, for the most part, committed herself to Victor's first-person narration) to allow the voices of other characters to interrupt and alter Victor's highly subjective account of the novel's events.

Victor's reaction to the letter reveals a great deal about his character. Though he is wracked with grief, his thoughts soon turn to his own anxiety at returning to his home after so long an absence. His self-absorption begins to seem impenetrable to the reader. Victor's uneasiness also foreshadows the moment of horror that greets him at Geneva; the reader has come to share his distress, and is thus as horrified as he by what the lightning illuminates.

The lightning storm that greets Victor is a staple of Gothic narrative. It evokes the classical (not to mention clichéd) preamble to any ghost story: "It was a dark and stormy night..." It also reflects the state of imbalance and chaos in which Victor finds his family. Though William's murder is described as taking place on an idyllic day in spring, it is chill and stormy when Victor arrives shortly thereafter.

Upon seeing the creature through Frankenstein's eyes, the reader is inclined to jump to the same conclusion that he does. Victor's hatred of the creature reaches an almost hysterical pitch in this scene, as is indicated by his diction: he refers to his creation as a "deformity," a "wretch," a "filthy demon." The reader, too, immediately wishes to blame the creature even though we have no real grounds for doing so. The reader is thus made subtly complicit with the creature's outcast state.

Victor's decision to keep the monster's existence a secret in order to preserve his reputation reveals him as both selfish and foolhardy. A child has been killed, and a monster brought to life: in a world so severely out of balance, Frankenstein's reputation ought be the furthest thing from his mind.

Chapter 8:

The trial commences the following morning. Victor is extremely apprehensive as to what the verdict will be: he is tortured by the thought that his "curiosity and lawless devices" will cause not one death, but two. He mournfully reflects that Justine is a girl of exceptional qualities, destined to lead an admirable life; because of him, her life will be cruelly foreshortened. Victor briefly considers confessing to the crime, but realizes that, as he was at Ingolstadt on the night of the murder, his confession would be dismissed as the ravings of a madman.

In court, Justine stands calmly before her accusers; her solemn face lends her an exquisite beauty. The prosecutor brings forth a number of witnesses, who provide compelling evidence against her: she was out for the whole night on which the murder was committed; she was seen near to the spot where the body was found; when questioned, she gave a confused and unintelligible answer; and she became hysterical at the sight of William's body. The most damning piece of evidence, however, is the fact that William's miniature, which he had been wearing at the time of the murder, was found in the pocket of Justine's dress.

Justine, called to the witness stand, provides another account of the events: with Elizabeth's permission, she had passed the night of the murder at her aunt's house in Chêne. Upon hearing of William's disappearance, she spent several hours searching for him; unable to return home, as it had grown too late, she determined to spend the night in a nearby barn. Justine says that if she was near the body, she did not know it; her confusion was only a manifestation of her tiredness. She remains unable to explain how the picture came to be on her person; she can only assume that the murderer himself placed it there.

Though few witnesses are willing to come forth to aver Justine's innocence, Elizabeth insists on speaking on the girl's behalf. She praises Justine's character, and says that she was beloved by the entire Frankenstein family; Elizabeth, for he part, will never believe that Justine is guilty. Despite this brave display of loyalty, Justine is condemned to death. Victor considers Justine's plight to be less than his own she is consoled by the fact of her own blamelessness, while he must live with his guilt.

Shockingly, Justine confesses to the murder, and expresses a wish to see Elizabeth, who asks Victor to accompany her. Justine tells them that she confessed to a lie in order to obtain absolution and avoid excommunication in her last moments. She does not fear death, and nobly spends her last moments in comforting Elizabeth and Victor. This only serves to heighten Victor's anguish, and he reflects that Justine and William are the first victims of his "unhallowed arts."

Analysis:

The minute attention paid to Justine's appearance, history, and speech only serves to heighten the sympathy felt by the reader. Her impassive countenance recalls that of a fragile doll: like a doll, she is a mere plaything, a pawn whose fate is entirely beyond her control. Throughout Chapter 8, the sentences are confused, and semicolons are frequently used to connect disjointed thoughts. In this way, Shelley indicates the magnitude of the chaos that has befallen the Frankenstein household: they have lost all control over both the present and the future, and are even unable to organize their own thoughts.

Though the reader might be tempted to hold Victor responsible for the verdict, this is an overly simplistic view of events. Frankenstein's decision to conceal the truth is terribly misguided; Shelley, however, gives us no indication that he does this in order to absolve himself of guilt. "Fangs of remorse" tear at him, and, in his own heart at least, he bears the guilt for both William's murder and Justine's execution. He can share his terrible secret with no one, and is thus utterly isolated, an outcast from human society.

Frankenstein Chapters 9-12 Summary and Analysis

Chapter 9:

Victor is tormented by the false calm that descends upon the Frankenstein household following the death of Justine. He is wracked with guilt; though he intended to further the cause of human happiness, he has ended in committing "deeds of mischief beyond description horrible." Victor's health suffers as a result of his massive sense of guilt and the bleak depression that accompanies it. His father, observing his misery, becomes ill as well.

The Frankenstein family, "blasted" as a result of their recent misfortunes, retires to their summer home at Belrive. There, Victor passes most of his hours in solitude; the fact that he must keep his role in William's death a secret makes the company of his family agonizing to him. He finds himself in extreme disharmony with the landscape of Belrive, which impresses him with its beauty and serenity. He often contemplates suicide, but is deterred by thoughts of Elizabeth's grief; he also fears the untold havoc his creature could wreak in his absence. Victor's hatred of the creature reaches pathological proportions, and takes on the character of an obsession; he thinks of nothing but his eventual revenge.

Elizabeth, too, is much changed by the tragedy; she has lost faith in the essential goodness of both humanity and the world as a whole. Now, men appear to her "as monsters thirsting after each other's blood." She does, however, persist in her fervent belief in Justine's innocence; she feels great pity for the man who must carry the guilt for William's murder on his conscience. Victor despairs when he hears her say this, as he feels that he is the man who must bear that guilt.

He seeks escape from his misery by traveling through the Alpine valley of Chamonix, in which he had often vacationed as a boy. Victor is awestruck by the overwhelming grandeur of the landscape, and views it as proof of the existence of an omnipotent god. The hard physical exercise exhausts him, and he is able to take refuge in sleep for the first time since the execution of Justine.

Analysis:

The reader cannot help but feel a certain ambivalence toward Victor's thoughts of suicide: while they reveal the magnitude and authenticity of his feelings of remorse, they also bespeak a certain selfishness. That he overcomes his desire to kill himself indicates that he is capable of mastering his self-absorption, at least occasionally: his concern for his family, and for the suffering that the creature could cause humanity as a whole, keeps him from the "base desertion" of suicide.

In this chapter, we see the dramatic effect that nature has upon Victor's well-being and state of mind. He praises nature for what he calls its sublimity that is, for the way in which it stands beyond the scope of human control and comprehension. This awestruck admiration is bitterly ironic, in light of the fact that Frankenstein's agony was originally caused by his desire to master nature and unlock its secrets. Nature, for Frankenstein, reveals the existence of an all-powerful god the very god whose works he attempted to improve upon and replace.

Elizabeth's apprehension of men as bloodthirsty monsters is quite significant: it highlights the ambiguous moral status of both Frankenstein and his creature. Who, Shelley insistently asks, is the true monster? Is it the creature that Victor abandoned? Or is it Victor himself, who obsessively fantasizes about taking his violent revenge upon the monster he himself created?

Chapter 10:

Victor continues to wander aimlessly in the valley of Chamonix, taking great consolation in the magnificence of the natural landscape. At the same time, he notes that the landscape is characterized by disorder and destruction: constant avalanches plague the valley, and it often seems that the mountains themselves will crash down on Victor's head.

Victor determines to climb to the top of Montanvert, one of the region's forbiddingly massive glaciers. The sight of the mountain fills him with a "sublime ecstasy"; he believes that human contemplation of natural wonders "gives wings to the soul and allows it to soar from the obscure world to light and joy." He is filled with melancholy as he ascends the mountain, however, and, amid rain and rockslides, meditates on the impermanence of all human dreams and attachments. When he has reached the summit, Victor invokes all the "wandering spirits" of the dead, and asks them to either permit him to be happy or carry him to his grave.

As if summoned by this call, the monster appears. Victor rains curses upon him and threatens to kill him, but the creature remains unmoved. He says that he is the most wretched and despised of all living things, and accuses his creator of a gross disregard for the sanctity of life: how else could Victor propose to murder a creature which owes its existence to him? The monster asks Frankenstein to alleviate his misery, and threatens to "glut the maw of death... with the blood of [Victor's] remaining friends" if he does not comply with his wishes.

The monster eloquently argues that he is intrinsically good, full of love and humanity; only the greatness of his suffering has driven him to commit acts of evil. Though he is surrounded by examples of human happiness, he finds himself excluded, through no fault of his own, irrevocably excluded from such bliss. He implores Frankenstein to listen to his story; only then should he decide whether or not to relieve the creature of his agony.

Analysis:

Victor's sojourn in the valley of Chamonix reveals his desire to escape the guilt he bears for the recent tragedies. There, he seeks oblivion in sleep, and in the bleakness of the glacial landscape. The chaos of that landscape, in which avalanches and rockslides are a constant threat, suggests that Victor's escape from his responsibility will be short-lived; it also foreshadows further tragedy.

The encounter between Victor and his creature is charged with Biblical allusions: like God and Adam, the creature's creator has cast him out. For him, Frankenstein occupies the position of the Christian god. The creature is also subtly aligned with the figure of Satan, or the devil: like him, he is a "fallen angel," grown brute and vicious in the absence of his god.

Shelley suggests that the creature's misdeeds are caused by the enormity of his suffering; at heart, he is essentially good and, more importantly, essentially human. If he is monstrous, no one but Frankenstein is to blame. When the outraged creature demands of his creator an answer to the question "How dare you sport thus with life?", the sentiments of the reader manifest. Frankenstein, in his hypocrisy, longs to murder a being that owes its life to him. If the creature is, paradoxically, both inherently good and capable of evil, then his creator is as well.

Chapter 11:

The creature has only the most vague memory of his early life: he recalls being assailed with sensory impressions, and was for a long time unable to distinguish among light, sound, and smell. He began to wander, but found the heat and sunlight of the countryside oppressive; he eventually took refuge in the forest near Ingolstadt, which offered him shade. The creature found himself tormented by hunger, thirst, and bodily pain. Only the light of the moon consoled him, and he grew to love the sound of birdsong. When he attempted to imitate it, however, he found the sound of his own voice terrifying, and fell silent again. With the same ecstatic astonishment that primitive man must have felt, the creature discovers fire.

All of the people that the creature encounters in his travels regard him with horror: he is often pelted with stones and beaten with sticks, though he attempts to make overtures of friendship. He finally comes upon a miserable hovel; this is attached to a cottage of poor but respectable appearance. Exhausted, he takes refuge there "from the inclemency of the weather and from... the barbarity of man." The creature, in observing the cottage's three inhabitants, contrives a great affection for the beauty and nobility of their faces. They an old man, a young man, and a young woman enthrall him with the sound of their music and the cadence of their language, which he adores but cannot understand.

Analysis:

This chapter is told from the creature's point of view. In this way, Shelley humanizes the creature: his first-person narration reveals him as a character of surprising depth and sensitivity. The reader becomes familiar with his trials and sufferings; we realize that, at the time of Frankenstein's abandonment, the creature was as innocent and defenseless as a human infant.

Like an infant, he is plagued by blurry vision, confusion of the senses, and an aversion to direct light: he experiences the world precisely as a young child would experience it. His syntax, as he begins describing his early life, is almost painfully simple. He is as yet incapable of interpreting or analyzing the world and his perceptions of it.

The creature's narrative voice is surprisingly gentle and utterly guileless: one of the most poignant moments in the novel is when the creature, despised by Victor and feared by the rest of mankind, collapses and weeps out of fear and pain.

In all of his encounters with humanity, the creature is met with horror and disgust. In the face of such cruelty, the reader cannot help but share the creature's fury and resentment: though he means no harm, his unbeautiful appearance is enough to make him a wretched outcast. He is, through no fault of his own, deprived of all hope of love and companionship; the reader thus slowly begins to sympathize with his desire to revenge himself on both his creator and on brutal humanity as a whole. As the novel progresses, we become more and more uncertain as to who is truly human, since the creature's first-person narration reveals both his own humanity and his creator's concealed monstrousness.

Chapter 12:

The creature begins by recalling his deep and tormenting desire to speak to the cottagers, who impress him with their gentleness and simplicity. He hesitates, however, as he is fearful of incurring the same kind of disgust and cruelty that he experienced at the hands of the villagers.

In observing the family, he discovers that they suffer from great poverty. The two young people are very generous with the old man, and often go hungry so that he might eat. The creature, greatly touched by this, ceases to take from their store of food, even though he is terribly hungry himself. He begins to cut their firewood for them, so that the young man, whose name is Felix, will no longer have to.

The creature spends the entire winter watching the cottagers, and grows to love each of them passionately. He attempts to learn their language, which he regards as "a godlike science." At first, he makes little progress. Every act of the cottagers, however banal, strikes him as miraculous: to watch them read aloud, or play music, or simply speak to one another, delights him immeasurably. Though he realizes that they are terribly unhappy, he cannot understand why: to him, the family seems to possess everything one could want: a roof, a fire, and the glories of human companionship.

Upon seeing his own reflection in a pool of water, the creature becomes even more certain that he will never know such happiness: he finds his own face to be monstrous, capable of inspiring only fear or disgust. Nonetheless, he dreams of winning the love of the cottagers by mastering their language; in this way, he hopes, he can reveal to them the beauty and gentleness of his soul.

Analysis:

This chapter details the creature's deep longing to join human society. He is, at first, utterly ignorant of the ways of humanity, and must learn everything from scratch. In essence, he is still a child, with all of a child's innocence and capacity for wonder. To him, the cottagers are god-like, blessed, despite the extreme humbleness of their existence.

In comparing himself to them, the creature feels himself to be a monster: he is shocked by his own reflection, and is nearly unable to accept it as his own. At the same time, he still dreams of acceptance into human society, and attempts to master language in order to inspire the family's affection and trust. The reader cannot help but pity the creature, and fear for him: we know too well that human society obstinately refuses to accept those who are different, regardless of the beauty of their souls. At chapter's end, the reader can only wait uneasily for the moment when the creature will present himself to his beloved family.

Frankenstein Chapters 13-16 Summary and Analysis

Chapter 13:

At the outset of spring, a stranger an exquisitely beautiful young woman of exotic appearance appears at the family's cottage. Felix is ecstatic to see her, kisses her hands, and refers to her as his "sweet Arabian"; later, the creature learns that her true name is Safie.♡

The creature notes that her language is different from that of the cottagers, and that the four humans have great difficulty in understanding one another. They communicate largely through gesticulation, which the creature is initially unable to interpret; he soon realizes, however, that the cottagers are attempting to teach Safie their language. He secretly takes part in her lessons and, in this way, finally begins to master the art of speech.

The book, from which Safie's lessons are taken, called the *Ruins of Empires*, provides the creature with a cursory knowledge of history. He grows to understand the manners, governments, and religions of modern Man, and weeps over the atrocities that human beings commit against one another. Upon hearing of man's obsession with wealth and class, the creature turns away in disgust; he wonders what place he can have among such people, since he owns no property, and is absolutely ignorant of the circumstances of his birth.

The creature curses his newfound knowledge, which has caused him to regard himself as a monster and an outcast. He despairs of ever gaining the fellowship of his beloved cottagers, as he is certain that they will recoil from his hideous appearance. At chapter's end, he is friendless, loveless, and almost completely without hope.

Analysis:

The language of Chapter 13 is extremely baroque, and lends the landscape a romantic, unreal quality: skies are described as "cloudless"; there are "a thousand scents of delight, and a thousand sights of beauty"; Safie is not merely brunette, but has "shining raven hair." This sort of diction elevates seemingly ordinary events to the level of the spectacular: it reveals the extent to which the creature idealizes the cottagers and all that is associated with them. He worships them, and longs for their love and acceptance. The creature's essential humanity now becomes clear to the reader: he feels sympathy, affection, and desire; he is capable of aesthetic appreciation (as we see in his enjoyment of the family's music); he has mastered language; and he is capable of self-analysis and reflection.

In referring to the Ruins of Empires, Shelley subtly reminds the reader of the ways in which humanity itself is monstrous: people commit unspeakable violence against one another, and exploit those who do not possess the trivial virtues of money and noble birth. The creature's horror at these revelations reveals his essential goodness; it also serves to echo the terrified disgust with which the villagers met his own deformity. Once again, Shelley forces us to reconsider the question of monstrousness here, it seems that it is the neglectful and selfish Frankenstein, and not his suffering creation, who truly deserves to be called a monster.

With the creature decrial of his own knowledge, he and Frankenstein become more closely aligned in the reader's mind; indeed, they are nearly indistinguishable. Both creator and creation are made outcasts by what they know; both long for nothing so passionately as they do their former innocence.

Chapter 14:

Some time elapses before the creature learns the family's history. Their surname is De Lacey, and they are the last of a noble French family. Only a few months previously, they had lived in Paris; there, they were surrounded by luxury and a glittering coterie of friends and intimates. They had, however, suffered a great misfortune, which forced them to go into exile.

The cause of this unhappy upheaval was Safie's father, a wealthy Turkish merchant who had been unjustly imprisoned by the Parisian government. All of Paris knew that racism, and a hatred of the merchant's Islamic faith, were the true cause of his incarceration. Felix, appalled by this injustice, went to the merchant's cell and vowed to do everything in his power to liberate him. To encourage the young man, the merchant promised Felix the hand of his beautiful daughter in marriage. The two young people fell in love immediately upon seeing one another, and eagerly looked forward to their union.

The merchant, however, loathed the idea of his cherished daughter marrying a Christian, and conceived a plan to betray Felix and take his daughter with him to Turkey. Safie, for her part, did not wish to return to her native land: her mother had been a Christian, and she longed for the greater freedom enjoyed by women in the countries of Europe.

Felix freed the merchant the night before his scheduled execution. As Felix was conducting the two fugitives across the French countryside, the French government threw Agatha and the elder De Lacey into prison. Felix, hearing of this, immediately decided to return to France, and asked the merchant to lodge Safie in Italy until such time as he could meet her there.

In Paris, the De Laceys were stripped of their ancestral fortune and condemned to live in exile for the rest of their lives. The treacherous merchant did nothing to help them, and in this way did the De Laceys come to live in the miserable German cottage in which the creature had found them.

The merchant, afraid of being apprehended, was forced to suddenly flee Italy. In her father's absence, Safie promptly decided to travel to Germany, where she was reunited with her lover.

Analysis:

The creature introduces this chapter as "the history of my friends"; it reveals his deep attachment to the family, and the meticulous attention he paid to every word they said. He tells Frankenstein that he transcribed the letters that Felix and Safie exchanged, and wrote down the family's story in order to remember it more exactly; it is clear that he regards the history of the world and the history of the De Laceys as being equally important.

The De Laceys' story illustrates both the goodness and evil of which mankind is capable more importantly, it shows the way in which each person may be capable of both good and evil. Felix's strong sense of justice leads him to aid the merchant; his love for his family draws him back to Paris, despite the fact that he knows that he will face a stiff punishment. By contrast, the merchant who is himself a victim of bigotry and hatred betrays the man who risked his life to help him. The creature thus encounters the two contrary aspects of human nature.

Of course, Shelley's representation of the Muslim merchant as lying and duplicitous is itself an example of nineteenth-century racism. By the same token, Safie's nobility of spirit is presumed to come from her Christian mother; the underlying assumption here is that Muslims, and Turks, are not capable of human kindness.

Chapter 15:

From the history of the cottagers, the creature learns to admire virtue and despise vice. His education is greatly furthered by his discovery of an abandoned leather satchel, in which he finds three books: Milton's *Paradise Lost*, *Plutarch's Lives*, and Goethe's *Sorrows of Werter*. He regards these books as his treasures, and they are of infinite importance to him: they alternately transport him to the highest ecstasy and cause him the most crushing despair.

The creature is enthralled with Werter's meditations upon death and suicide; with Plutarch's elevated regard for the heroes of past generations; and with the grand themes presented in *Paradise Lost*. He reads all of the books as though they were true histories, and regards Milton's story of the struggle between God and his creations as completely factual. In his mind, the biblical story defines his own. He does not see himself as Adam, however, but as Satan: unlike Adam, he is alone, without a Creator to protect him or an Eve to sustain him. He is full of envy, wretched, and utterly an outcast.

Soon after the discovery of the satchel, the creature finds Frankenstein's laboratory journal; from it, he learns the circumstances of his creation. He curses his creator and the day he received life; he grieves over his own hideousness and despairs of ever finding human companionship. The creature bitterly reflects that even Satan is more fortunate than he: at least Satan has fellow devils to console him. He, by contrast, has no one; his increasing knowledge only serves to make him more aware of his wretchedness. He is, however, still able to retain his hope that the cottagers will recognize his virtues and overlook his deformity -- if only he can bring himself to speak to them.

With the arrival of winter, the creature finally determines to speak to the cottagers: he reasons that he is not unworthy of love and kindness, and that the De Laceys are compassionate enough to offer it to him. He decides to speak to the senior De Lacey at a time when the other cottagers are away. The old man, who is blind, will be better able to appreciate the mellifluousness of his speech and the genuine goodwill in his heart; the young people, by contrast, would be horrified at the very sight of him. He hopes to gain their trust by first gaining the trust of their respected elder.

Though the creature's dread of rejection nearly paralyzes him, he at last summons all of his courage and knocks upon the De Laceys' door. After a fraught silence, the creature bares his soul to the old man: he tells him that he is a wretched outcast, and that the De Laceys are his only friends in the entire world. De Lacey is astonished, but Safie, Felix, and Agatha burst into the cottage before he can reply to the creature's entreaty. The women scream in terror, and Felix, in a "transport of fury," violently beats the creature with his walking stick. The creature, his heart still full of love for the De Laceys, cannot bring himself to retaliate. Instead, he flees the cottage and takes refuge in his hovel.

Analysis:

The creature's discovery of the satchel of books is one of the most significant events in the novel. *Sorrows of Werter* and *Paradise Lost* are arguably two of the greatest books in the history of world literature: they thus serve as examples of the highest beauty which mankind is capable of producing. Similarly, *Plutarch's Lives* exalts the work of heroes, thereby providing another illustration of human virtue and accomplishment.

While the satchel furthers the creature's knowledge of civilization, and of the triumphs and sufferings of men, it also, in his own words, teaches him to "admire the virtues and deprecate the vices of mankind." One might describe this as a moral education; that is, the creature comes to distinguish between good and evil, and to look upon the former as preferable to the latter. Paradise Lost is the most important of the three books with regard to the creature's burgeoning morality. Milton's poem concerns itself with the struggle between God and the Devil, which is, at least in the Western imagination, the most important, most epic battle between the forces of good and evil.

The fact that the creature regards the books (all of which are fictional) as true histories illustrates that his childlike credulity and innocence has survived his early suffering. And yet, the books themselves shatter that innocence: through them, he feels the tragedy of his predicament for the first time. He feels himself to be forsaken, and cannot decide if he is most like Adam or most like Satan: he decides upon the latter because he is so much an outcast, completely without guidance or protection.

The struggle between good and evil described in *Paradise Lost* is also an allegory for the struggle within each human being, and within the creature himself. At this point in the narrative, warring impulses vie with one another for the creature's soul: will he behave as a man, or as a monster?

By the end of the chapter, the reader is not certain which of his impulses will prevail. As Felix is mercilessly beating him, the creature is unable to lift his hand against him: in this way, the reader sees the creature's innate humanity. If he later behaves as a monster, the reader cannot help but understand why: he has been terribly abused and reviled by those people whom he loved and trusted best. Despite his essential goodness, he is hated, and so he can only hate mankind in return.

Chapter 16:

The creature curses his creator for giving him life. Only his great rage, and his consuming desire for revenge, keeps him from taking his own life: he longs to "spread havoc and destruction around [him], and then to [sit down] and enjoy the ruin."

He falls upon the ground in utter despair and, at that moment, declares war upon all mankind for its callousness and cruelty. He vows to exact revenge upon his creator the man who "sent [him] forth into this insupportable misery."

With the arrival of morning, the creature allows himself to hope that all is not lost: perhaps he can still endear himself to the elder De Lacey, and thereby make peace with his children. When he returns to the cottage, however, he finds it empty. He waits, tortured by anxiety, until Felix finally appears in the company of a strange man. From their conversation, he learns that the De Laceys have determined to leave the cottage out of fear that he (the creature) will return.

The creature cannot believe that his protectors, his only connection to humanity, have abandoned him. He spends the remains of the day in his hovel, by turns weeping and feverishly contemplating the revenge he will take upon mankind. By morning, he is overcome with fury, and burns down the cottage in order to give vent to his anger.

The creature decides to travel to Geneva in order to revenge himself upon his creator.

The journey is long and arduous, and the weather has grown bitterly cold. Though he primarily travels by night, in order to avoid discovery, he permits himself to travel during daylight on one of the first days of spring. The new warmth soothes him, and the sunlight revives some of his former gentleness. For a few precious moments, the creature "dares to be happy."

At length, a young girl comes running through the forest, and he hides himself beneath a cypress tree. As he watches, she suddenly stumbles and falls into the rapidly moving water; the creature, without thinking, leaps in and rescues her from certain death. As he is attempting to revive her, a peasant (presumably the girl's father) snatches the girl away from him, and shoots the creature when he attempts to follow. The creature bitterly contemplates this "reward for [his] benevolence," and is seized with a new, even greater hatred of humanity.

Shortly thereafter, he arrives in Geneva. Once again, a child runs past his hiding-place in the deep woods. The creature is much taken with the beautiful child, and speculates that he is still too young to feel hatred for his deformity. He seizes the boy's arm as he runs past; the child screams in terror and struggles to get away. He calls the creature a "hideous monster," and says that his father, M. Frankenstein, will punish him. Upon hearing the name of Frankenstein, the creature, enraged, strangles him. He feels a "hellish triumph" at the boy's death, and reflects that his despised creator is not, after all, invulnerable.

The creature takes the necklace, as he finds the picture of Caroline exquisitely beautiful. At the same time, the image fills him with redoubled fury, for no one will ever look upon him with the divine kindness he sees in Caroline's eyes.

Seeking a hiding place, he enters a nearby barn and finds Justine sleeping within. Her beauty, too, both transports him to ecstasy and fills him with bitter despair, since he will never know the pleasures of love. Suddenly terrified that she will awake and denounce him as a murderer, he places the portrait of Caroline in Justine's dress: she, not he, will suffer punishment for the murder. In his madness, the creature thinks that it is the inaccessible beauty of people like Justine that caused him to kill William; it is thus only fair that she should atone for the crime.

At the end of his tale, the creature commands Frankenstein to make him a companion "of the same species and of the same defects," so that he will no longer be so miserably alone.

Analysis:

The idea of fire is pivotal to Chapter 16. When the creature sets the cottage on fire, it is as though he were giving vent to "the hell he [bears] within [himself]" a hell that hearkens back to that described by Milton in *Paradise Lost*, as we saw in the previous chapter. The fire consumes the cottage with its "forked and destroying tongues"; this image alludes to both the fires of hell and the forked tongue of Satan, who took the form of a snake when he appeared to Adam and Eve in the Garden of Eden.

The weather both reflects and determines the creature's mental state: when the De Laceys abandon him, it is winter, and the countryside is barren and desolate. The heavens pour rain and snow, and violent winds ravage the landscape: these natural phenomena serve as symbols for the fury that the creature intends to unleash upon the world. With the arrival of spring, he finds himself filled with joy and benevolence. His encounter with the girl and her father is thus bitterly ironic: at a moment in which the creature permits himself to be happy, and to hope for an end to his sufferings, he is once more confronted with people's unreasoning horror of him. The fact that he saves the child from certain death indicates that, at least at this moment, he still has sympathy for mankind; if he loses it afterwards, the reader can scarcely blame him.

It is important to note that the creature's murder of William and mistreatment of Justine are the result of his longing for human connection. Upon seeing William, he wishes to keep the boy as his companion; the sight of Justine fills him with love and desire. He can have neither of them; neither is willing to overlook his external ugliness. It is therefore only fitting that he should end his tale by asking Frankenstein to make him a female companion, since all of his crimes arise out of his crushing loneliness. The narrative seems to suggest that isolation so total would drive anyone mad; the creature thus cannot be held entirely responsible for his actions.

Frankenstein Chapters 17-20 Summary and Analysis

Chapter 17:

Frankenstein resumes his narration at the start of this chapter. Bewildered by the creature's story and enraged by his account of William's death, Victor initially refuses to create a female companion for him. He argues that their "joint wickedness" would be enough to destroy the world. The creature replies by saying that he is only malicious as a result of his misery: why should he meet man's contempt with submission? If he is met with hatred, he can only respond in kind. He appeals to Victor for sympathy, and asks Frankenstein to provide him with a lover to share in his suffering. If he complies, the creature promises to quit the company of mankind forever.

Frankenstein cannot help but see the justness of this argument. Though he feels a certain compassion for the creature, the "loathsomeness" of his appearance soon replaces his sympathy with horror and hatred. The creature continues to plead, saying that his "vices are the children of a forced solitude"; in the company of another his virtues would come forth, and he would thus become "linked to the chain of existence and events" from which he is now excluded.

Victor is torn. He thinks of the creature's supernatural strength, and about the great destruction he still might cause. He therefore determines to comply with the creature's request, in order to save both his family and the rest of humanity. The creature says that he will anxiously observe his progress and then leaves him. Victor descends the mountain with a heavy heart, and returns to Geneva haggard.

Analysis:

The most important feature of this chapter is the way in which the creature convinces Frankenstein to comply with his request. Throughout the better part of their exchange, the creature's tone is reasonable in the extreme: in fact, his desire for a companion seems almost noble. In this way, he will divest himself of his longing for violence and revenge, and lead a blameless life.

By aligning his maliciousness with his misery, he is implicitly blaming Frankenstein for what he has become: such an accusation, however, is effective in evoking the sympathy of both Victor and the reader. The creature often refers to Frankenstein as "you, my creator": this doubled form of address does not only serve to remind Victor of the responsibility he bears for giving the creature life; it is also a complimentary title that implores him for help.

As he speaks, the creature's syntax becomes almost Biblical in tone: he frequently uses the verb "shall," which has the ring of both prophecy and command. He is thus subtly informing Victor that he has no choice in this matter: his acquiescence is already a foregone conclusion.

Chapter 18:

Weeks pass, and Victor cannot bring himself to begin his work. Though he fears the creature's wrath, his abhorrence for the task proves insurmountable. He realizes that several months of study are required before he can begin composing the second creature; he determines to study in England, as the discoveries of an English philosopher will prove essential to his research. He endlessly delays asking his father for permission to do so, instead electing to remain in Geneva. His home is greatly beneficial to his health and spirits, and he has once again grown strong and cheerful. When his melancholy overtakes him (as it inevitably does), he takes refuge in solitude, and his good humor is soon restored.

The elder Frankenstein, who has observed these changes with pleasure, takes Victor aside and asks him about his recent desire for solitude. He wonders if Victor has perhaps decided that he does not wish to marry Elizabeth, but has not told his father out of fear of disappointing him. Victor reassures him that nothing could be further from the truth: he longs to marry Elizabeth, but must first satisfy a desire to visit England. The idea of marrying his beloved with his hateful task still uncompleted is unbearable to him. Victor disguises his true reasons for going abroad to his father, and the elder Frankenstein immediately consents to his request. It is decided that he and Elizabeth are to be married immediately upon his return to Geneva.

Henry Clerval is enlisted to accompany Victor on his journey; Victor is initially displeased at this, as he had wanted to undertake his task in perfect solitude. He is thrilled upon seeing Clerval, however, and reflects that Henry's presence will keep the creature from observing the progress of his work.

Though Victor is haunted by the fear that the creature will wreak havoc upon his family in his absence, he recalls that the creature has vowed to follow him wherever he might go. He abhors the idea of traveling in the monster's company, but realizes that it will ensure the safety of his loved ones. At this moment, he feels himself to be "the slave of [his] creature."

Victor and Clerval meet at Strasbourg, and travel by boat through Germany and Holland, and thenceforth to England; they arrive at London in December.

As he recalls their journey, Frankenstein is struck by the great difference between Clerval and himself. Clerval was entirely alive to the natural landscape, which he loved with unparalleled ardor; Victor, by contrast, was wracked with melancholy, and felt himself a "miserable wretch." Victor mourns over the memory of Clerval, whom he still considers a man of peerless worth and beauty of soul.

Analysis:

Victor's decision to marry Elizabeth immediately upon returning from England seems foolhardy: he has no way to know what will become of his pact with the creature. The marriage, for both Victor's father and Victor himself, represents the fulfillment of all the family's hopes and expectations: it will serve to restore order to the Frankenstein household after the terrible events that have befallen them. The union of Elizabeth and Victor will affirm that nothing has changed, that life continues as usual: it thus serves as a blatant affront to the creature's desire to revenge himself upon his creator. Indeed, marriage can only be grossly offensive to the creature, which has been deprived of all hope of love and companionship. It is important to note that Victor's marriage is dependent upon the creature: that is, he and Elizabeth will only be united if the creature is given his mate.

Frankenstein's happiness, at this point in the novel, is inextricably bound up with that of his creation; thus he feels himself to be the creature's slave. The two are now doubles for each other: like the creature, Victor suffers from an impenetrable solitude; like him, his romantic happiness is dependent upon the compassion of another; like him, he feels himself to be a "miserable wretch" unfit for human society. The question of who is the creator, who the creation will only become more confused as the novel builds to its inevitable conclusion.

Victor's questionable sense of ethics re-emerges in his decision to conceal his true reasons for journeying to England. He openly expresses fear that he may be exposing his family to danger and yet he never thinks to alert them to the threat. No reason is provided to account for this deliberate omission. The reader can only take it as yet another illustration of the narrator's selfishness; the fact that he ends the chapter by speaking of Clerval in the past tense, as a mere memory, foreshadows the catastrophic consequences that this deception will have.

Chapter 19:

In London, Clerval occupies himself with visits to learned and illustrious men; Victor cannot join him, however, as he is too absorbed in the completion of his odious task. He reflects that the trip would have given him indescribable pleasure while he was still a student; now, however, he wants only to be alone, as "an insurmountable barrier has been placed between [him] and [his] fellow men."

To Victor, Clerval is the image of his younger self: he is full of excitement and curiosity, and is at present making plans to travel to India. The two men receive a letter from a mutual friend inviting them to visit him in Scotland; though Victor detests all human society, he agrees to go, so as not to disappoint Clerval. He also looks forward to seeing the mountains once more.

The pair sets out for Scotland at the end of March. Victor reflects that he was "formed for peaceful happiness," having spent his youth in the enjoyment of nature and the contemplation of human accomplishment. Now, he feels himself to be a "blasted tree," an example of wrecked and forsaken humanity.

Clerval and Frankenstein spend time at Oxford, where they wonder over English history; for a brief moment, Victor "dares to shake off his chains" and is nearly happy. Almost immediately, however, he recalls his task, and is cast back into his former despair.

The pair finally arrives in Scotland. Victor is overcome by fear that he has neglected his work too long, and that the creature will visit his wrath upon his family or his friend. He awaits his letters from Geneva with tormenting anxiety, and follows Henry about as though he were his shadow.

After visiting Edinburgh and a number of other cities, Victor leaves Henry, having resolved to finish his work in a remote part of the Scotch countryside. His friend urges him to hurry back, as he will grow lonely without Victor's company.

Frankenstein devotes most of his mornings to labor, and walks the bleak and stony beach at night. His horror at his task increases daily, in stark contrast to the enthusiasm with which he undertook his first experiment. He grows progressively more anxious and terrified that he will meet his monster. He looks upon the new creation with a mixture of hope and "obscure forebodings of evil."

Analysis:

The symbol of the blasted tree is crucial to understanding what Frankenstein has become. A tree is a living organism that branches and spreads itself widely. One that is "blasted" is split down the middle, severed from its roots, unable to register sensations. The happiness that Victor once so casually enjoyed is now tainted by memories of the past and visions of the future. He can no longer find solace, since his soul cannot take pleasure in the manner it once did.

Frankenstein says that a "bolt" (as of lightning) has entered his soul. The reader cannot help but recall that the creature was brought to life by means of lightning: once again, Victor and his creature have become inextricably entangled. Both are separated from humanity by, in Victor's words, "an insurmountable barrier": for the creature, that barrier is his ugliness; for Frankenstein, it is his guilt. Victor's journey through Northern Europe seems to be a condensed version of the creature's own journey: both reflect on how they were once able to find consolation in nature and stories of human accomplishment (recall the creature's discovery of the satchel of books); now, nothing can ease their suffering.

The Scotland in which Frankenstein undertakes his second experiment is "a desolate and appalling landscape"; it thus mirrors the desolation and horror in Victor's heart. At chapter's end, the reader shares in the narrator's "forebodings of evil."

Chapter 20:

It is night. Frankenstein sits in his laboratory, contemplating the possible effects of this second experiment. He becomes increasingly horrified by his task and finds himself tormented by a number of questions: will this second creature be even more malignant than the first? Will she, unlike her mate, refuse to quit the company of man? Will they ultimately despise each other's hideousness as a mirror of their own? Frankenstein is repulsed by the thought that the two monsters might beget children and thereby create a new race that could ultimately destroy all humanity. Victor decides that unleashing such a scourge upon mankind would be of the utmost selfishness.

He glances up at the window to see the creature grinning at him from behind the glass. As the monster looks on, Frankenstein tears the half-finished creation to pieces. The creature howls in fury and despair, and then disappears.

Several hours later, the creature visits Victor while he is sitting in his laboratory lost in dreary contemplation. The creature reproaches him with having broken his promise, and asks if all his hardship and suffering has been for naught. When Frankenstein vows never to create another being like him, the creature calls him his "slave" and reminds him: "You are my creator, but I am your master." Seeing that Frankenstein will not be moved by threats, the creature swears that he will have his revenge upon his creator; he leaves him with a chilling promise: "I will be with you on your wedding-night."

Frankenstein passes a sleepless night; he weeps at the thought of how great Elizabeth's grief would be if her lover were to be murdered. He resolves not to fall before his enemy without a struggle.

A letter arrives from Henry, begging his friend to join him in Perth, so that they might proceed southward together. Victor decides to meet him in two days time. While disposing of the remnants of his second creation, Victor is overcome with disgust; he feels as though he has desecrated living human flesh. He resolves to dispose of the remains at sea.

At about two in the morning, Victor boards a small skiff and pilots it far away from shore. He disposes of the remains, and sails onward; he soon grows tired, however, and falls asleep in the bottom of the boat.

Upon awakening, Victor is terrified to find that his fragile ship has drifted into treacherous water. He thinks of how his death would leave his family at the mercy of the creature; the thought is torture to him, and he is nearly driven mad by it. Despite his misery, Victor still clings to life: he rejoices when he is out of danger, and manages to arrive safely on Irish shores.

A crowd of people observes his approach with suspicion; they rain verbal abuse upon him and cry that he is a villain. A bewildered Frankenstein is told that he must go see the magistrate, as he is suspected of being responsible for the death of a man who was found murdered the previous night.

Analysis:

Victor's decision to abandon his second experiment fills the reader with ambivalence. While he seems to be motivated by humanitarian concerns, it is also clear that he will expose his family and friends to grave danger if he does not comply with the creature's request. This possibility, however, appears not to have occurred to Victor: he inexplicably assumes that the creature's wrath will be visited upon him, and not upon Elizabeth, on his imminent wedding-night. The reader, however, can only expect the reverse: in destroying his second creation, he has destroyed the creature's bride and any chance the creature might have of happiness; the creature, we imagine, will respond in kind.

The creator and his creation continue to uncannily double one another, though their relation is now hopelessly confused: Victor is now the creature's "slave," and his life is entirely of the creature's design. It is no longer clear who is the creator, who the creation; who is the father, and who the child.

Of course, Victor's relation to the creature is closer to that of a mother than that of a father: it is, after all, a mother who "bodies" a child forth. Victor now stands in a subordinate position with relation to his creature a position that is fraught with implications of femininity. Some commentators have read the creature's promise "to be with [Victor] on his wedding-night" as a sexual threat, a means of claiming Victor's body as well as his soul. The film version of Frankenstein, directed by James Whale, also interprets this threat as a sexual one; Whale, however, regarded the relation between the creator and his creation as homoerotic. If the creature places himself between Victor and Elizabeth (and if Victor places himself between the creature and his bride), they do so in order to have each other all to themselves. The monster, like Stevenson's Mr. Hyde, can be regarded as the wicked part of Victor's own character; it has been tiresomely common for critics and readers to regard homosexuality as the most evil act of which man and the creature could be capable.

Victor's near-death at sea is strangely ironic: Frankenstein might have perished, thereby robbing the creature of his longed-for vengeance. In this way, he could have escaped the creature and saved his defenseless family; instead, he stubbornly clings to life and, miraculously, is able to pilot the boat to shore. The narrative suggests that Frankenstein's fate lies in his creation's hands: he will not be spared the final catastrophe.

Frankenstein Chapters 21-24 Summary and Analysis

Chapter 21:

Victor is brought before the magistrate, and several witnesses testify against him. A crew of local fishermen found the victim, a young man of about twenty-five years of age. When Victor hears that the victim was strangled, he trembles with anxiety; this, he knows, is his creature's preferred modus operandi.

Seeing Frankenstein's agitation, Mr. Kirwin, the magistrate, suggest that Victor be shown the body, so that the tribunal might judge his reaction. Frankenstein is well composed as they conduct him toward the room in which the body has been laid; he has an unassailable alibi for the time that the body was found. When he walks into the chamber, he is overcome with horror: the lifeless form of Henry Clerval lies before him. Frankenstein throws himself upon the body, and becomes almost mad with grief and guilt; he is carried from the room in convulsions.

For two months, Victor lies in a delirium of fever and confusion. He cries out that he is a murderer, and begs his attendants to aid him in apprehending the monster. He often imagines that he feels the hands of the monster closing about his neck, and starts from his bed in an agony of terror.

Victor longs for death, and finds his ability to survive such an epidemic of tragedies bitterly ironic. He concludes that he was, after all, "doomed to live."

When Victor finally emerges from his delirium, he finds that a grim-faced old woman has been attending upon his sickbed. She tells him that he will be sorely punished for the murder that he has committed, and would be better off dead; she seems to take pleasure in her own hatefulness and cruelty. The physician who is sent to examine Victor is equally careless and unfeeling. Victor bitterly reflects that now only the executioner is concerned with his well-being.

Frankenstein learns that Mr. Kirwin alone has shown him great kindness during his sickness; it is he who provided Victor with his sickroom and doctor. The magistrate visits him and expresses confidence that he will be cleared of all responsibility for the murder. He tells Victor that "a friend" has come to see him; thinking that it is the monster, Victor begs to have him sent away. Mr. Kirwin, much taken aback by this outburst, sternly informs him that the visitor is his father; at this, Victor is overjoyed.

He immediately asks after the safety of Elizabeth and Ernest, and the elder Frankenstein assures him they are all well. At the mention of Clerval, Victor weeps and exclaims that a horrid destiny hangs over his head.

His father's presence is "like that of a good angel" for Victor; slowly, he begins to regain his health. He often wishes that he were dead, but imagines that it is some dark force that keeps him alive, so that his evil destiny might be fulfilled.

Though Victor is cleared of all criminal charges, as "the cup of life [is] poisoned forever." His father tries in vain to cheer him, but Victor suffers from an insuperable melancholy. He is under constant observation, so as to keep him from taking his own life.

At length, Victor determines to triumph over "selfish despair," so that he might return to Geneva to protect his remaining family. Though the elder Frankenstein wishes to postpone the journey until his son has recovered from his melancholy, Victor will not be dissuaded. He cannot sleep without the aid of laudanum (a tranquilizer), and is frequently tormented by nightmares in which his creature strangles him.

Analysis:

There is a certain irony in Victor's being cleared of murder. On the one hand, he does bear some of the responsibility for Henry's death, insofar as it was he who created the monster; on the other, he was committing murder (of a kind) on the night in question. Recall that he was disposing of the female creation's remains at sea while the monster was strangling his friend. It might be said that Victor murdered that second creature; Henry's death can thus be regarded as his punishment for doing so.

The secret of the creature's existence is becoming too much for Victor to bear; he accuses himself of murder (albeit while in a semiconscious state) and tells his father that there is a nightmarish destiny that he has yet to fulfill. Victor longs to supersede the barrier of secrecy that has been erected between him and the rest of humanity. Here, we can see that he has forsaken his former selfishness: though he often longs for death, he forces himself to overcome this self-serving impulse in the hopes of keeping his surviving family from harm.

The death of Clerval serves as a symbol for the death of the last of Frankenstein's romantic idealism. It was Henry who helped to focus Victor's attentions on the world beyond the purview of science; it was he who enabled Victor to delight in the simple pleasures of nature. Victor is now deprived of even that joy, since he no longer has the privilege of seeing the world through Clerval's eyes. With each new murder, a piece of Frankenstein dies as well. He becomes increasingly broken, and is tormented by hysterical fits and fevers. Each of his attempts to withdraw into death or madness is thwarted, however: Victor is "doomed" to stay alive until his destiny has been completed.

Chapter 22:

Victor and his father are forced to stop in Paris, as Victor has grown too weak to continue the journey. The elder Frankenstein urges him to take solace in society. Victor, however, cannot bring himself to comply: the company of people is abhorrent to him. Though he is full of a great and indiscriminate love for humanity, feeling them to be "creatures of an angelic nature and celestial mechanism," he does not feel himself worthy of sharing in their intercourse. He has created a being who delights in bloodshed, and thus deserves only abhorrence and hatred.

Victor tells his father that he is the true engineer of all the catastrophes that have befallen them, but Alphonse attributes his confession to delirium. When his father begs him not to say such dreadful things, Victor replies that he would gladly have died in their place, but that he could not sacrifice all humankind to save those whom he loved. At length, Frankenstein is able (albeit through "the utmost self-violence") to control his desire to declare his guilt to the world.

He receives a letter from Elizabeth, who says that she is longing to see him. She expresses regret that he has suffered so terribly, and tells him that if his unhappiness is related in any way to their impending marriage, she will gracefully leave him to the arms of another.

Victor is reminded of the creature's threat to be with him on his wedding night. He decides that if the creature succeeds in murdering him, he will at last be at peace; if, on the other hand, he triumphs, he will be able to enjoy both freedom and life with Elizabeth.

As Frankenstein wants desperately to please both Elizabeth and his father, he decides that he will not delay the marriage any longer than is necessary: after all, the creature has demonstrated, by the murder of Clerval, that he will not be kept from violence before the fateful wedding.

At Geneva, he finds Elizabeth much changed by all that is happened. She has lost the vivacity of her youth, but Victor regards her, in her new compassion and gentleness, as an even more fitting companion "for one so blasted and miserable" as he.

He often feels that he will succumb to madness; at these times, only Elizabeth can soothe him. Frankenstein promises her that he will reveal the reason for his misery on the day after their wedding.

His father urges him to let go of his unhappiness. Though their circle has grown small, it will be bound more closely together by mutual misfortune, and, in time "new objects of affection" will be born to replace what has been lost.

Victor and Elizabeth look forward to their union with both pleasure and apprehension. The necessary preparations are made, and the couple determines to honeymoon on the shores of Lake Como, in Italy. Victor takes a number of precautions to protect both himself and his beloved; he becomes accustomed to carrying pistols and daggers about his person wherever he goes.

As the wedding-day approaches, the threat seems to be almost a delusion; Victor allows himself to believe that the marriage will actually take place, and that he will at last know happiness. Elizabeth seems cheerful, but is seized with melancholy on the day that the wedding is to take place. Victor now regards her sadness as a presentiment of evil, and imagines that she was apprehensive to discover the reason for his misery.

All is perfect on their wedding day. It is to be the last happy day in Victor's life. As they land on the shores of Como, both Elizabeth and Victor are overcome by a sense of inexplicable foreboding.

Analysis:

The hastiness of Victor's wedding is indicative of his frantic desire to create an illusion of order and tranquility for his family. The narrator vows not to "delay the moment a single hour." His urgency fills the reader with an almost unbearable apprehension, since we realize that Victor is hurtling toward the consummation of his horrible destiny. For Alphonse and Elizabeth (and even, to some extent, for Victor himself), the event appears to be a means of safeguarding the future. Elizabeth and Alphonse cling to the idea of the marriage as to a raft at sea; they hope to salvage something of happiness from the senseless and unremitting tragedy.

Elizabeth, for her part, finds her joy commingled with an inexplicable foreboding of misfortune; in this way, Shelley foreshadows her doom. Victor seems to have temporarily lost the ability to reason; the decision to marry despite the creature's threat is nearly mad in its recklessness. In telling the story to Walton, he remarks that the creature "as if possessed of magic powers... had blinded him [Victor] to his real intentions." By this point in the novel, the creature has taken on supernatural proportions: it is as though he were the unleashed wrath of hell itself. Thus the earthly weapons that Frankenstein carries to protect himself against the creature seem futile in the extreme.

Significantly, Frankenstein compares himself and Elizabeth to Adam and Eve. He says that his "paradisiacal dreams of love and joy" are dashed by the realization that "the apple was already eaten, and the angel's arm bared to drive [him] from all hope." This Biblical allusion has a number of ramifications. The apple of which Eve ate came from the Tree of Knowledge, which God had forbidden them to touch; it was for their curiosity that the first people were cast out of Paradise. Similarly, Frankenstein's misfortune befell him as a result of his overweening scientific curiosity and his desire to defy the work of God.

Frankenstein is aligned with both Adam and Eve, and, implicitly, with the creature himself: recall that the creature briefly compared himself to Adam during his reading of Paradise Lost. Strangely, this metaphor also serves to put the creature in the place of both God and the angel; he is thus positioned as the creator of Frankenstein himself. Their roles are now reversed.

Chapter 23:

Night has fallen by the time Victor and Elizabeth land on the shores of Como. The wind rises with sudden violence, and Frankenstein becomes increasingly anxious: he is certain that either he or his creature will die tonight. Elizabeth, seeing his agitation, implores him to tell her what it is he fears. Though he attempts to console her, he cannot bring himself to reply to her question; he says only that it is a dreadful night.

Hoping to spare Elizabeth from the sight of the monster, Victor asks her to retire to her bedchamber. She complies, and Victor stalks the corridors of their villa, searching for any trace of the monster. At length, he hears a dreadful scream; too late, Victor realizes the enormity of his mistake.

Upon entering the bedroom, he finds Elizabeth lying strangled upon the bed, her clothes and hair in a state of disarray; the print of the monster's fingers are still fresh upon her neck. Unable to tolerate the shock, he collapses.

When he revives, he finds himself surrounded by the people of the inn; he escapes from them to the room in which Elizabeth's corpse is lying. He falls upon her body and takes it in his arms. Wracked by indescribable grief, he looks up to see the monster grinning at him through the windowpane. Victor fires his pistol, but the creature eludes him.

Frankenstein alerts the other guests of the murderer's presence, and they try in vain to apprehend him. Though he longs to aid them in their search, he is feeble as a result of his shock and misery; he is carried, barely conscious, to his bed. Realizing that he does not know whether his father and brother are safe, Victor gathers all of his strength and travels to Geneva. On the journey, he reflects that he has lost all hope of future happiness; no being in all creation is so miserable as he.

Though both Alphonse and Ernest are safe when Victor arrives, the former soon perishes upon hearing of the death of Elizabeth. Victor has no memory of the time that immediately followed the death of his father; he later learned that he was kept in a miserable asylum, having been declared mad.

Upon his release, all Victor is obsessed by thoughts of taking revenge upon his creature. He visits a magistrate to ask for the help of the law in apprehending the creature. Though the official listens attentively, it is clear that he only half-believes Frankenstein's wild tale. He tells Victor, quite reasonably, that it would be nearly impossible to pursue a superhuman being of the kind he has described. Frankenstein is enraged, and vows that he will devote himself to the creature's destruction. He recognizes his lust for vengeance as a vice but says that, in his current state of wretchedness, it is "the devouring and only passion of his soul."

Analysis:

Once again, the natural landscape foreshadows impending violence: upon the arrival of the Frankensteins, the wind at Como grows violent and a storm arises. Predictably, nature has lost its power to reassure; now, it reflects the chaos and darkness that Victor carries.

There is great irony in Victor's inability to recognize the monster's true intentions. The reader knows that it is Elizabeth, and not Frankenstein, who will bear the brunt of the monster's wrath; there is thus great pathos in Victor's horror at his mistake. The guilt he feels at Elizabeth's death is twofold: he both created her destroyer and left her completely unprotected at the moment of her death.

Victor is now indistinguishable from his creature: both are utterly bereft, loveless, and alone. Both are sustained only by their desire to revenge themselves upon the other. In their hatred for one another, they are more closely bound together than ever before.

Chapter 24:

Frankenstein has lost the capacity for voluntary thought; his entire consciousness is occupied by fantasies of revenge. He resolves to leave Geneva forever because the country has become hateful to him in the absence of his loved ones. Taking a sum of money and his mother's jewels, he goes off in search of the monster.

Before leaving Geneva, however, he visits the graves of his family. He kisses the earth and vows to avenge their deaths; he calls upon "the wandering ministers of vengeance" and upon the spirits of the dead to aid him in his quest. Suddenly, Victor hears a "fiendish laugh," as though hell itself were mocking him. From out of the darkness, the creature whispers that he is "satisfied" that Frankenstein has determined to live.

For months, he pursues the creature over the better part of the earth. At times, he is guided in his search by peasants who have been frightened by the hideous apparition; at others, the creature himself leaves Frankenstein some clue of his whereabouts, so that Victor will not despair and abandon his quest. Victor feels that some good spirit protects him throughout this journey; it alone saves him from death. He has grown to despise his life, and only finds refuge in sleep; in dreams he is once again among his beloved dead.

The creature cuts taunting messages into trees and stones, in order to remind his creator of the absolute power he has over him. He provides Frankenstein with food and advises him to prepare himself for the intolerable cold of the North: it is into these icy wastelands that the creature intends to lead him. Though Frankenstein knows that this final journey will mean certain death, he pursues the monster without hesitation.

Upon seeing the creature traversing the ice on a dogsled, Frankenstein weeps tears of hope and joy. When he has almost overtaken his enemy, however, he inexplicably loses all trace of him. Shortly thereafter, the ice breaks apart, and Victor is set adrift on a single jagged floe. He is on the brink of death when Walton's ship appears in the distance.

Though Victor looks forward to the peace that death will bring him, he despises the idea of dying with his task is unfulfilled. He begs Walton to kill the creature if he shows himself to him no matter how eloquent and persuasive he seems.

Analysis:

Strangely enough, this final chapter of Victor's narration, in which he is suffering a decline, finds him more dynamic than he has been since the days of his first experiment. Revenge invigorates him, intoxicates him: the joy he feels at seeing the creature's sledge marks the first time he has been happy in innumerable months.

Frankenstein liberates himself from his prison of guilt, opting instead for one of wrath. In a certain sense, the creature has finally succeeded in gaining the companionship he always desired. Frankenstein is doomed to share the creature's life, and to follow him wherever he may go: the two are as close as a parent and child, or a lover and his beloved. It no longer matters who occupies which position: each reciprocates the obsession of the other.

The chase appears almost childish: the creature taunts his creator, and Frankenstein pursues him with no regard for sense or reason. If nothing else, it presents Frankenstein with a challenge; it once again calls forth the lust for conquest that motivated his scientific endeavors. The creature is his master, his leader, and his animating force. Now it is the monster that brings his maker to life: without his desire for revenge, Frankenstein would surely have died long ago.

Frankenstein Walton, continued Summary and Analysis

Walton, continued:

Walton fondly recalls Victor's face, its shifting expressions; he remembers how his "fine and lovely eyes" were, by turns, filled with indignation, sorrow, and wretchedness. Walton is extremely curious as to how Victor was able to generate life; when questioned, however, Victor becomes extremely agitated. He entreats Walton to learn from his miseries, rather than endeavoring to create new ones; he says that, "like the archangel who aspired to omnipotence" (i.e., Satan), he "is chained in eternal hell."

Upon learning that Walton has prepared a written account of his history, Frankenstein corrects and augments it; he primly remarks that he does not want a "mutilated version to go down to posterity." With each successive conversation, Walton grows fonder of Victor, whose eloquence and erudition never fail to impress him; he feels that he has found the beloved friend whom he has always been seeking. Victor thanks him for his affection, but says that no new tie can replace the ones that he has lost.

In subsequent letters to his sister, Walton writes of the dire danger in which he and his crew find themselves. Mountains of ice surround them, and it is not clear whether they will be able to free themselves; if, by a miracle, they are saved from death, the crew wants to return to England. Many of them have already died of cold and frostbite.

Walton hesitates, unwilling to grant their request. Even though he is in a half conscious state, Victor rouses himself enough to chastise the men for wishing to abandon their "glorious expedition." He tells them that they will be hailed as "benefactors of the species...brave men who encountered death for honor and for the benefit of mankind" if they continue with their expedition; to turn back would be pure cowardice, unbefitting a man. The men are unable to reply, and Victor lapses back into sleep.

The men remain firm in their demands, however, and Walton consents to return to England. He is bitterly disappointed to have lost his dreams of glory. When Walton informs Frankenstein that he is determined to head south, Victor says that he, unlike Walton, will not abandon his quest. He attempts to leap out of bed, but is too weak to do so; the doctor who is summoned to examine him says that he only has a few hours left to live.

On his deathbed, Victor says that he finds his past conduct to be blameless; he entreats Walton, "in perfect reason and virtue," to pursue the creature's destruction after his death. In a rare moment of sanity, he tells the young captain to avoid ambition; only a moment later, however, he reconsiders, and says that Walton may succeed where he himself failed. With that, he dies.

At midnight on the evening of Frankenstein's death, the creature steals into the ship to view the body of his dead creator. He utters exclamations of grief and horror, but moves to escape when Walton walks into the chamber. Walton asks him to stay. The creature, overcome with emotion, says that Victor, too, is his victim; he asks Frankenstein to pardon him for his crimes. Despite all that has transpired between them, the creature still harbors love for his creator.

Walton regards the creature with a mixture of curiosity and compassion, but cannot bring himself to console him. The creature says that it caused him agony to commit his crimes, since his heart "was fashioned to be susceptible to love and sympathy": only the greatness of his misery drove him to vice and hatred. Walton, though he is touched by the creature's remorse, still feels great indignation at his crimes: he says that the creature has "thrown a torch into a pile of buildings, and when they were consumed...sat among the ruins and lamented the fall."

The creature ruefully remarks that he did not expect to find any sympathy from Walton, but is content to suffer alone. He cannot believe that he is the same being who once dreamed of sublime beauty and transcendent goodness; now he is "the fallen angel become a malignant devil." He wonders why Walton does not despise Felix, or the rustic who sought to kill the savior of his child; the monster feels itself to be "an abortion, to be spurned at, and kicked, and trampled on." Walton's hatred of the creature cannot, however, equal the creature's hatred of himself; the creature says that he will throw himself upon a funeral pyre, and thus be saved from the enormity of his remorse. With that, he leaves the ship, and is "lost in darkness and distance."

Analysis:

In death, Frankenstein appears to have learned nothing at all from his sufferings. He still wants posterity to revere and remember him, as is indicated by his augmentation of Walton's written account of his tale. He commands Walton's men to continue their expedition, thereby endangering their own lives and the lives of their fellow men; it is clear that the pursuit of fame and glory is still foremost in his mind. Recall that he, too, once longed to "benefit the species" through scientific enterprise; his creature -- and all the havoc his creature wrought -- was the result.

Even at the moment of his death, Victor displays an unparalleled selfishness: he asks Walton to continue the quest for vengeance that has brought Victor himself to such ruin, and tells him that he need not forsake his outsize ambitions. Frankenstein, though we pity him for all he has lost, remains irredeemably arrogant, and seems to regard human life as being ultimately less valuable than pioneering endeavor. Walton, for his part, has learned little from Frankenstein's tale: he is consumed with curiosity about how one might generate life, and bitterly laments the termination of his voyage.

It is important to note that both Frankenstein and his creature compare themselves to Satan in this final chapter: both feel they have fallen from a great height to end in ruin and decay. Once again, they are indissolubly linked it is as though they have become the same person. It is therefore only logical that the creature should die now that Frankenstein is dead: he has lost his animating principle, the person who made his life worth living.

We discover that the creature did not relish his crimes; instead, they were abhorrent to him; he is wracked (as his creator was) with guilt and self-hatred. His last description of himself is as an "abortion," a metaphor that is of the utmost significance: the creature does not feel that he has ever truly lived. Like an aborted child, he was unwanted by his parent, and was never permitted to fully develop: he is a monster, not-quite-human, but with the capacity for humanness. This creature, which has been said to carry hell within itself, chooses to die by fire; in this way can he completely destroy the body that was so hated by so many.

Frankenstein Symbols, Allegory and Motifs

Allegory: Prometheus

As discussed in Major Themes, Victor Frankenstein is allegory for the mythical figure, Prometheus. As the latter stole fire from the gods and was punished for it, so did the former discover the secret to creating life, and subsequently suffer for it.

Motif: poetry

Shelley intersperses quotations from and references to poetry throughout the novel, adding a level of artistic awareness to a novel that purports to be testimonial in nature.

Allegory: Genesis

Frankenstein's creation of the monster can be read as an allegory for the creation story from Genesis, of God creating Adam. As is the case in that story, Frankenstein forms the creature in his image (i.e., that of a human -- albeit grotesquely), and animates the creation.

Motif: letters

The novel is deeply concerned with evidence and direct testimony with respect to events. As such, proof of communication between people is often conveyed in the form of letters, both within the story (e.g., the monster showing letters from his upbringing to Frankenstein) and in a reflexive context (i.e., the most direct interface between the reader and narrative is the collection of Walton's letters to his sister).

Motif: retrospection

The novel is explicitly retrospective on every level: Walton is recounting events that have already happened in his letters to his sister; Frankenstein is recounting his history to Walton; the monster is recounting his past to Frankenstein. As such, the tone of the narrative is generally very self-aware and reflective -- expressing regret over what happened; imagining how events might have gone differently; and so forth.

Frankenstein Metaphors and Similes

"He came like a protecting spirit to the poor girl, who committed herself to his care" (Volume I, Chapter 1) (Simile)

Like the common expression of someone being a "guardian angel," this simile compares Frankenstein Senior's compassion and caring for Caroline to the image of a blessed spirit aiding her.

"The saintly soul of Elizabeth shone like a shrine dedicated lamp in our peaceful home" (Volume I, Chapter 2)" (Simile)

Here, Frankenstein compares the compassion and moral goodness of Elizabeth to a holy light banishing darkness.

"[In] drawing the picture of my early days, I also record those events which led, by insensible steps, to my after tale of misery: for when I would account to myself for the birth of that passion, which afterwards ruled my destiny, I find it arise, like a mountain river, from ignoble and almost forgotten sources; but, swelling as it proceeded, it became the torrent which, in its course, has swept away all my hopes and joys" (Volume I, Chapter 2) (Simile)

Frankenstein compares his fascination with reanimation to a mountain river: like a river, it has a unique source (alchemy books and his father's disapproval); like a river, it has a current in which he was swept up and pulled towards his destiny.

Simile - "Sir Isaac Newton is said to have avowed that he felt like a child picking up shells beside the great and unexplored ocean of truth" (Volume I, Chapter 2).

Frankenstein uses this simile to express the sentiment of childlike curiosity, humility, and wonderment that (according to Newton) comes with learning small truths about the vast universe through science.

"What had been the study and desires of the wisest men since the creation of the world was now within my grasp. Not that, like a magic scene, it all opened upon me at once: the information I had obtained was of a

nature rather to direct my endeavours so soon as I should point them towards the object of my search, than to exhibit that object already accomplished. I was like the Arabian who had been buried with the dead, and found a passage to life, aided only by one glimmering, and seemingly ineffectual, light" (Volume I, Chapter 4) (Simile)

According to Frankenstein, his pursuit of knowledge over the mastery of life was slow, piecemeal, and tedious, like a man navigating a dark tunnel using a single, minuscule light.

Frankenstein Irony

The monster's grotesqueness

Frankenstein's aim was to create a beautiful creature; yet the reality of his creation was out-of-joint with this goal, and he ultimately created something grotesque. He describes this when he recounts the creation event to Walton: "How can I describe my emotions at this catastrophe, or how delineate the wretch whom with such infinite pains and care I had endeavoured to form? His limbs were in proportion, and I had selected his features as beautiful. Beautiful!--Great God! His yellow skin scarcely covered the work of muscles and arteries beneath; his hair was of a lustrous black, and flowing; his teeth of a pearly whiteness; but these luxuriances only formed a more horrid contrast with his watery eyes, that seemed almost of the same colour as the dun white sockets in which they were set, his shrivelled complexion and straight black lips" (Volume I, Chapter 5).

The monster's elocution

Largely due to the monster learning to read via *Paradise Lost*, he speaks in eloquent English, showing a mastery of language that one would not expect given his monstrous appearance and character.

Frankenstein's responsibility for William's death

Frankenstein sought to use science to create life; yet it was his very creation that led to the death of one of his own family members.

Progress as a destructive force

One would expect scientific progress to be socially productive; however, Frankenstein's 'achievement' of creating life leads only to death and suffering, both for his creation and the world around him.

Frankenstein Imagery

Psychological scenery

Particularly in Frankenstein's narration, the description of scenery often reflects his mental state at the time of the scene. Take, for example, the morning after he brought the monster to life and fled his home: "Morning, dismal and wet, at length dawned, and discovered to my sleepless and aching eyes the church of Ingolstadt, its white steeple and clock, which indicated the sixth hour. The porter opened the gates of the court, which had that night been my asylum, and I issued into the streets, pacing them with quick steps, as if I sought to avoid the wretch whom I feared every turning of the street would present to my view. I did not dare return to the apartment which I inhabited, but felt impelled to hurry on, although drenched by the rain which poured from a black and comfortless sky" (Volume I, Chapter 5). The loss of night's 'asylum' and the dismal, wet weather both echo Frankenstein's weariness and anxiety.

The passage of time

Imagery techniques are used to focalize the passage of time. This is what happens when Frankenstein returns home from university following the death of William, and gazes upon a portrait of his mother: "Six years had elapsed, passed as a dream but for one indelible trace, and I stood in the same place where I had last embraced my father before my departure for Ingolstadt. Beloved and venerable parent! He still remained to me. I gazed on the picture of my mother, which stood over the mantel-piece. It was an historical subject, painted at my father's desire, and represented Caroline Beaufort in an agony of despair, kneeling by the coffin of her dead father. Her garb was rustic, and her cheek pale; but there was an air of dignity and beauty, that hardly permitted the sentiment of pity" (Volume I, Chapter 7). The past-focused imagery functions as a link between Frankenstein's history and what he must cope with in the present.

Bodily manifestations of emotions

Imagery and rich descriptive language bring the inner states of Frankenstein to life. Take, for instance, the moment after Justine was wrongly sentenced to death for the death of William, when Frankenstein is overcome by guilt for his own crime of creating the monster: "The blood flowed freely in my veins, but a weight of despair and remorse pressed on my heart, which nothing could remove. Sleep fled from my eyes; I wandered like an evil spirit, for I had committed deeds of mischief beyond description horrible, and more, much more (I persuaded myself), was yet behind" (Volume I, Chapter 9).

Sublime nature

The backdrop of nature, particularly in the scene prior to Frankenstein's mountaintop encounter with his monster, subsumes human nature within the grander, terrifying scope of the universe. This has a somewhat humbling, soothing effect on Frankenstein, as he notes in the passage prior to his encounter with the monster; "I [roamed] through the valley. I stood beside the sources of the Arveiron, which take their rise in a glacier, that with slow pace is advancing down from the summit of the hills, to barricade the valley. The abrupt sides of vast mountains were before me; the icy wall of the glacier overhung me; a few shattered pines were scattered around; and the solemn silence of this glorious presence-chamber of imperial Nature was broken only by the brawling waves, or the fall of some vast fragment, the thunder sound of the avalanche, or the cracking reverberated along the mountains of the accumulated ice, which, through the silent working of immutable laws, was ever and anon rent and torn, as if it had been but a plaything in their hands. These sublime and magnificent scenes afforded me the greatest consolation that I was capable of receiving. They elevated me from all littleness of feeling; and although they did not remove my grief, they subdued and tranquillised it" (Volume I, Chapter 10).

Frankenstein Free Will, Determinism, Culpability, Behaviorism

Have a seat Kermit. What I'm about to tell you might come as a big shock...

One of the particularly interesting aspects of *Frankenstein* is its exploration of free will and determinism. This debate, in broad terms, is the question of whether we are genuinely able to choose how we act, or if our actions are instead predetermined, entirely outside of our control. This is something that has been discussed by philosophers since ancient Greece; Shelley's novel uses science fiction to bring the debate into a modern context.

What makes the matter of free will and determinism particularly salient in *Frankenstein* is the fact that, by stipulation of the part of Frankenstein, the creation of his monster was entirely determined by him: he uncovered the precise scientific procedure underpinning each step up to the monster's creation. Such a procedural design of a living being makes it easy for us to draw the inference that the monster, as an entity, has been entirely architected by Frankenstein -- and, crucially, the monster is not ultimately *responsible* for his actions, since he could not choose otherwise.

It is true, of course, that the monster *learns* things after his creation; yet the story suggests that this learning process only further served to determine the behavior of the monster exogenously. Namely, the monster says that he learned how to feel and think about things through books -- *Paradise Lost, Plutarch's Lives*, and the *Sorrows of Werter*. So while Frankenstein may not be wholly responsible for the actions of his monster, it still does not seem that the monster is responsible for his actions.

This is another way in which the monster is made to seem conceptually distant from humanity: because the reader has knowledge of the invention of the monster, we can easily suppose his actions to be determined, and thereby view him much more as a high-functioning automaton than an extremely ugly human. Yet the novel makes this issue more complicated: though the monster may *seem* distinct from humanity for this reason, is this *actually* something that distinguishes him from humanity?

The parallelism at work in the novel suggests that humans may function in the same way as the monster. Both Frankenstein and the monster account for their actions by describing their origins and the different external forces that influenced them; the only difference is that we explicitly know that Frankenstein constructed the monster. Yet if we stop and consider Frankenstein, we know that he, too, was *created*: he was merely created by two parents instead of a single scientist. Is that difference conceptually significant? Perhaps not: in both cases, the science by which the organism was created largely determines, in conjunction with external influences, how the organism will behave.

This is essentially a thesis of behaviorism: the notion that people's actions are programmed based on a combination of their biology and environmental feedback. Nowadays, such a view is considered reductive with regards to human nature; but what *Frankenstein* importantly underscores is that there is at least *some* degree to which our actions are not conceived purely as a function of our own agency. People, literature, and our environment in general prompt us to act and think in particular ways -- and perhaps, as such, we ought to broaden our scope of precisely who and what is culpable for the actions of any one person.

Frankenstein Literary Elements

Genre

science fiction; horror

Setting and Context

Early 19th century Europe

Narrator and Point of View

There are three levels of first-person limited narration, with each successive level embedded in the immediately prior level. The first level is R. Walton, writing to his sister; the second is Frankenstein, speaking to Walton; the third is the monster, speaking to Frankenstein.

Tone and Mood

Because the horrific events of the story are conveyed as retrospection, the tone oscillates between remorse/anger on the part of the narrator, and suspense on the part of the reader for not having total knowledge of the events that will unfold, in spite of the narrator foreshadowing them.

Protagonist and Antagonist

The major protagonist is Frankenstein, and the major antagonist is his monster.

Major Conflict

Most of the conflict in the story can be read as a struggle of will between Frankenstein and his monster. The monster wants Frankenstein to make him a mate, and Frankenstein believes that he must destroy the monster in order to end the monster's destructive rampage.

Climax

Chronologically, the climax actually happens at the beginning of the text, when Walton encounters Frankenstein pursuing the monster in the direction of the North Pole.

Foreshadowing

The novel as a whole is rife with foreshadowing because of the narrators' retrospective perspective and disposition toward regret.

Understatement

The section of the book in which Frankenstein actually creates the monster is highly understated: very little time is spent on the explicit act of bringing the creature to life.

Allusions

The story alludes to Genesis, Prometheus, and various other literary texts. See the guide's section on allegory and motifs for more details.

Imagery

See the Imagery section of the guide.

Paradox

One of the primary threads in the book is that the scientific progress purported by Frankenstein actually effects pain and destruction, and might ultimately be socially regressive. Such a notion of 'progress' is paradoxical.

Parallelism

The ontology of the novel as a composite of older literary sources parallels the ontology of the monster as a composite of older, dead body parts.

Metonymy and Synecdoche

N/A

Personification

Nature as a force is often personified in the text. An example of this is when Frankenstein travels through the countryside following the execution of Justine: "The abrupt sides of vast mountains were before me; the icy wall of the glacier overhung me; a few shattered pines were scattered around; and the solemn silence of this glorious presence-chamber of imperial Nature was broken only by the brawling waves, or the fall of some vast fragment, the thunder sound of the avalanche, or the cracking reverberated along the mountains of the accumulated ice, which, through the silent working of immutable laws, was ever and anon rent and torn, as if it had been but a plaything in their hands" (Volume I, Chapter 10).

Frankenstein Links

E-text for Frankenstein

http://literature.org/authors/shelley-mary/frankenstein/

An online version of the novel, in its entirety.

A Dictionary of Greek and Roman biography and mythology, William Smith, Ed.: Prometheus.

http://www.perseus.tufts.edu/hopper/
text?doc=Perseus%3Atext%3A1999.04.0104%3Aalphabetic+letter%3DP%3Aentry+group%3L
bio-1

The mythological history of Prometheus.

Mary Shelley's Frankenstein

http://www.imdb.com/title/tt0109836/

IMDb page for the 1994 film adaptation of the novel.

Frankenstein Essay Questions

1. **Discuss similarities between Frankenstein's monster and the text of the novel as a whole.**

   Both the monster and the text of the novel are objects that have been created by salvaging older materials. In the case of the monster, Frankenstein built his body out of dead body parts; he also learned how to think, read, and speak from old literary texts. Similarly, the overall text is held together by references and allusions to various poems and literary works. As such, we see that both objects are something new that have been synthesized from a collection of old components.

2. **How might the novel be read as a commentary on scientific progress?**

   Frankenstein, a young scientist filled with ambition, becomes obsessed with the possibility to create life -- something that science has yet to accomplish. Ultimately, he is able to do so; through this act, he achieves what we would typically conceive of as 'scientific progress', because he has expanded the scope of what science allows humanity to do. However, this act of 'progress' has almost entirely negative consequences: the monster subsumes the entirety of Frankenstein's life, murders innocents, and achieves no perceptible good for society. One might say, therefore, that the novel reflects a thesis that not all potential scientific advancements are progressive of necessity.

3. **What relation does the novel's alternate title, _The Modern Prometheus,_ bear to the story?**

   Frankenstein is a Promethean analogue: just as Prometheus stole fire from the gods, so too did Frankenstein 'steal' from the domain of nature by learning the secret to create life by himself. Just as the gods for this crime punished Prometheus, Frankenstein receives nothing but misery from his creation, and ultimately dies in an attempt to destroy what he made. In this way, Shelley's novel really is a modern retelling of the Prometheus myth.

4. **What does the novel gain from having so many levels of narration? Why do you suppose it might have been structured with so many embedded narratives?**

   One noteworthy aspect that this structure affords the novel is that it adds to the parallelism between the monster and overall text. The novel is a patchwork of various perspectives and testimony, be they various narrators or the voices conveyed through various letters. This makes the overall narrative a dubious patchwork of the experiences of different people, similarly to the way in which the monster's body is literally composed of parts of many different deceased people.

This structure also creates a deep sense of irony within the text. It is a text overtly concerned with scientific standards of proof; however, the multiple narrators and secondhand information directly undercut the degree to which the reader has grounds to believe the narrative. Like the moral sphere of the narrative's events, this is a puzzle that the novel compels the reader to resolve.

5. **Do you think that the monster has free will? Provide textual examples in support of your claim.**

[Multiple answers can be argued. This is merely one example.]

Assuming the truth of Frankenstein's testimony, the monster does not have free will. Frankenstein says that "the stages of the discovery [with respect to learning how to give life to inanimate tissue] were distinct and probable," which implies that there was explicit scientific grounding for every aspect of the creation process (Volume I, Chapter 4). If we take this claim seriously, then we can plausibly infer that the underlying mechanisms of the monster's brain and body were entirely designed by Frankenstein -- whether or not Frankenstein was consciously aware of the ramifications of his design. With regards to the creatures mind, we know that the majority of his sentiments and schemas of thought were coopted from the three books by which he learned how to read -- *Paradise Lost, Plutarch's Lives,* and *The Sorrows of Werter*. We therefore have plausible grounds to claim that external forces ultimately determine all aspects of the monster's behavior.

Frankenstein Quizzes

1. **Robert Walton is a**
   A. Scientist
   B. Sea captain
   C. Doctor
   D. Merchant

2. **Walton's goal on his expedition is to**
   A. Find a new country
   B. Find the creature
   C. Find a passage between the Atlantic and Pacific
   D. Find gold

3. **Where does the expedition find Victor Frankenstein?**
   A. In a cave
   B. At the bottom of the ship, stowing away
   C. On a floating piece of ice in the ocean
   D. None of the above

4. **Who is Beaufort?**
   A. Victor's grandfather
   B. The dear departed friend of Victor's father
   C. The father of Caroline
   D. All of the above

5. **The marriage between Victor's parents comes about after**
   A. The move to Switzerland
   B. The death of Beaufort
   C. The birth of Victor
   D. The departure of Wallace

6. **Walton narrates the story and writes letters to**
   A. His aunt
   B. His fiancee
   C. His mother
   D. His sister

7. **Henry Clerval is**
   A. A relative of the Frankenstein family
   B. A professor
   C. A merchant
   D. Victor's closest childhood friend

8. **Who is Elizabeth Lavenza?**
  A. A girl taken in by the Italian peasant family
  B. The adopted daughter of the Frankensteins
  C. A serving girl
  D. both The adopted daughter of the Frankensteins and A girl taken in by the Italian peasant family

9. **Victor's initial interest in science is sparked at age 13 when he reads**
  A. The works of da Vinci
  B. The works of Cornelius Agrippa
  C. The works of Galileo
  D. The works of Plato

10. **At the University in Ingolstadt, Victor becomes interested in**
  A. Neither A nor B
  B. both Chemistry and The elixir of life
  C. The elixir of life
  D. Chemistry

11. **Caroline succumbs to**
  A. Polio
  B. Scarlet fever
  C. Diphtheria
  D. Chicken pox

12. **Ultimately, Victor's schooling results in his obsession for**
  A. Money
  B. Power
  C. Knowledge
  D. Supernatural

13. **Armed with scientific knowledge, Victor decides upon the artificial creation of**
  A. A human
  B. A monster
  C. A robot
  D. None of the above

14. **How often does Victor visit his family while in school?**
  A. Rarely
  B. Never
  C. Frequently
  D. Occasionally

15. **After Victor animates his creation, he**
>A. Meets Clerval the next morning
>B. Tries to hide
>C. Runs away
>D. All of the above

16. **The horror Victor feels at the creature's movement can be defined as**
>A. Reality crashing into dreams
>B. Knowledge crashing into dreams
>C. Reality crashing into knowledge
>D. A dream crashing into reality

17. **Clerval's original purpose in coming to the University is to**
>A. Nurse Victor's illness
>B. Study
>C. Go sightseeing
>D. Fetch Victor

18. **Caroline dies peacefully with the assurance of**
>A. A union between Victor and Justine
>B. A union between Ernest and Elizabeth
>C. A union between Victor and Elizabeth
>D. A union between Elizabeth and William

19. **The creature's chance encounter with William in the forest might be described as**
>A. The ends justify the means
>B. Irony
>C. both Poetic justice and Irony
>D. Poetic justice

20. **Victor and Henry learn of William's death via**
>A. Premonition
>B. Express messenger
>C. Letter
>D. Telegram

21. **Why is Justine accused of William's murder?**
>A. She confessed her guilt
>B. She was framed.
>C. both She was framed and The picture of Caroline was found in her dress
>D. The picture of Caroline was found in her dress

22. **After Justine's condemnation, in order to mitigate his guilt and sadness, Victor**
   A. Starts a new experiment
   B. Returns to Ingolstadt
   C. Spends time with his family
   D. Wanders the mountains and valleys

23. **When Victor meets up with his creation in the mountains, how much time has passed?**
   A. Four years
   B. A year
   C. Three years
   D. Two years

24. **Henry Clerval might best be described as**
   A. Cold and calculating
   B. Passionate and romantic
   C. Practical and intelligent
   D. Insensitive and callous

25. **Why does Victor remain in the creature's cave to hear his tale?**
   A. He hopes to hear that the creature was not responsible for William's death
   B. It is too cold outside
   C. He cannot find his way home
   D. He is scared to leave

Quiz 1 Answer Key

1. **(B)** Sea captain
2. **(C)** Find a passage between the Atlantic and Pacific
3. **(C)** On a floating piece of ice in the ocean
4. **(D)** All of the above
5. **(B)** The death of Beaufort
6. **(D)** His sister
7. **(D)** Victor's closest childhood friend
8. **(D)** both The adopted daughter of the Frankensteins and A girl taken in by the Italian peasant family
9. **(B)** The works of Cornelius Agrippa
10. **(B)** both Chemistry and The elixir of life
11. **(B)** Scarlet fever
12. **(C)** Knowledge
13. **(A)** A human
14. **(B)** Never
15. **(D)** All of the above
16. **(D)** A dream crashing into reality
17. **(B)** Study
18. **(C)** A union between Victor and Elizabeth
19. **(C)** both Poetic justice and Irony
20. **(C)** Letter
21. **(C)** both She was framed and The picture of Caroline was found in her dress
22. **(D)** Wanders the mountains and valleys
23. **(D)** Two years
24. **(B)** Passionate and romantic
25. **(A)** He hopes to hear that the creature was not responsible for William's death

Frankenstein Quizzes

1. **After being abandoned by his maker, the creature subsists on**
   A. Small animals
   B. Stolen food
   C. Roots and berries
   D. Tree bark

2. **The relationship between Victor and the creature can be likened to that between**
   A. God and Adam
   B. Esau and Jacob
   C. Jacob and Rachel
   D. Cain and Abel

3. **The creature takes refuge in a cave and spends his days**
   A. Watching a family of three
   B. Stealing
   C. Sleeping
   D. Mourning the loss of his maker

4. **When he observes the distress of the family, the creature leaves _____ on the doorstep.**
   A. Kindling
   B. Food
   C. Money
   D. Water

5. **Felix is thrilled with the arrival of**
   A. Safie
   B. De Lacey
   C. the creature
   D. Agatha

6. **The family relationship is best defined as**
   A. A father, a son and a daughter
   B. A mother, a son and a daughter
   C. A mother and two sons
   D. A father and two daughters

7. **The creature might best be described as**
   A. Completely cruel
   B. Completely helpless
   C. Cruel at times but misunderstood
   D. Unintelligent

8. **Clerval is murdered by the creature when Victor**
   A. Refuses to make another creature
   B. Returns to Switzerland
   C. Runs away
   D. Decides to pursue another experiment

9. **The major driving forces behind the creature's destructive behavior are**
   A. Vengeance
   B. Kindness
   C. both Vengeance and Loneliness
   D. Loneliness

10. **Victor is acquitted of the charge of Clerval's murder because of**
    A. His own testimony
    B. The influence of his father
    C. His horrified reaction upon seeing the body
    D. An eyewitness

11. **The creature is able to kill Elizabeth because**
    A. Elizabeth invited him inside
    B. The creature was hiding under the bed
    C. Victor left the bedroom to stand guard outside
    D. None of the above

12. **The entire novel can be viewed as a cautionary tale about**
    A. Religion
    B. Wealth
    C. Curiosity
    D. Intelligence

13. **In the end, who knows of the creature's origin and existence?**
    A. both Victor and Walton
    B. Victor
    C. Neither A nor B
    D. Walton

14. **Victor's painful story is not in vain because Walton**
    A. Records it for publication
    B. Promises to kill the creature
    C. Turns back from the dangerous expedition
    D. None of the above

15. **The story concludes when the creature**
    A. Takes over Walton's ship
    B. Kills Victor
    C. Mourns Victor and pledges his own death
    D. Is arrested by the police

16. **'Science' in Shelley's context refers to**
      A. most usually biology
      B. most ususaly chemistry
      C. what we now consider STEM fields
      D. learning and knowledge in a broad sense

17. **The philosopher stone was thought to**
      A. turn any metal into gold or silver
      B. make its user immortal
      C. convince people of anything
      D. manipulate time

18. **A 'syndic' is another term for**
      A. someone who is doubtful of many things
      B. a consiprator
      C. a chief magistrate
      D. a lawyer

19. **Parallelism exists most strongly between the text as a whole and**
      A. the monster
      B. William
      C. Frankenstein
      D. Walton

20. **There are many instances in the text of**
      A. stream-of-consciousness narrative
      B. sexual manipulation
      C. creation events
      D. divorce

21. **There are _ major levels of narrative in the story.**
      A. 3
      B. 2
      C. 4
      D. 1

22. **When Frankenstein encounters Walton, he believes that his ultimate destiny is to**
      A. create a mate for the monster
      B. kill the monster
      C. revive William
      D. kill himself at sea

23. **The narrative focuses on the _____ of events.**
      A. random happenstance
      B. irrelevance
      C. mystery
      D. causal dependency

24. **Frankenstein is an analogue for**
      A. Zeus
      B. Macbeth
      C. Prometheus
      D. Adam

25. **The major theme most pertinent to the setting of the North Pole is**
      A. causal dependency
      B. literary reflexivity
      C. isolation
      D. creation

Quiz 2 Answer Key

1. **(C)** Roots and berries
2. **(A)** God and Adam
3. **(A)** Watching a family of three
4. **(A)** Kindling
5. **(A)** Safie
6. **(A)** A father, a son and a daughter
7. **(C)** Cruel at times but misunderstood
8. **(A)** Refuses to make another creature
9. **(C)** both Vengeance and Loneliness
10. **(C)** His horrified reaction upon seeing the body
11. **(C)** Victor left the bedroom to stand guard outside
12. **(C)** Curiosity
13. **(A)** both Victor and Walton
14. **(C)** Turns back from the dangerous expedition
15. **(C)** Mourns Victor and pledges his own death
16. **(D)** learning and knowledge in a broad sense
17. **(A)** turn any metal into gold or silver
18. **(C)** a chief magistrate
19. **(A)** the monster
20. **(C)** creation events
21. **(A)** 3
22. **(B)** kill the monster
23. **(D)** causal dependency
24. **(C)** Prometheus
25. **(C)** isolation

Frankenstein Quizzes

1. **A major aspect of morality brought into question by the narrative is**
    A. nihilism
    B. natural law
    C. Kantianism
    D. marketplace ethics

2. **One could say that Frankenstein is enslaved to his monster because**
    A. the monster holds hm captive for a period of 18 months
    B. he believes that destiny binds him to his monster
    C. he is forced to make a mate for the monster
    D. the monster ultimately murders him

3. **Frankenstein's own childhood is _____ the monster's 'childhood'.**
    A. virtually the opposite of
    B. foreshadowing of
    C. identical to
    D. the inspiration for

4. **Frankenstein blames _____ for provoking his path to alchemy.**
    A. his father
    B. his mother
    C. his sister
    D. the government

5. **Frankenstein tends to tell the story of his path through life in terms of**
    A. whatever details will best allow Walton to recreate his monster
    B. what he thinks Walton wants to hear
    C. destiny
    D. choices he made as an individual

6. **Frankenstein is invested in**
    A. killing Walton
    B. providing his audience with verification of his story
    C. preparing his last will
    D. building a mate for his monster

7. **Frankenstein's reticence towards explaining the mechanism of animating dead tissue conveys**
    A. an interest in protecting the monster
    B. distrust of Walton
    C. narrative unreliability
    D. mental illness following the death of William

8. **Frankenstein explicitly aims to avoid _____ in his narrative**
   A. evidence
   B. sentimentality
   C. moralizing
   D. science

9. **When the monster first saw Frankenstein, he**
   A. fled from him
   B. screamed
   C. smiled
   D. spoke his name

10. **Both Frankenstein and his monster based much of their identity on**
   A. books
   B. astrology
   C. Frankenstein's father
   D. science

11. **In the monster's final monologue, he laments that he never found**
   A. God
   B. justice
   C. his origins
   D. the copy of Paradise Lost that he read as a 'child'

12. **Prometheus famously**
   A. flew too close to the sun
   B. slept with Hera
   C. slept with his own mother
   D. stole fire from the gods

13. **Shelley builds her novel in part around**
   A. references to poetry
   B. allusions to The Last Supper
   C. undertones of black magic
   D. foreshadowing of a dystopian totalitarian regime

14. **Frankenstein's scientific achievement can be seen as allegory for**
   A. the raising of Lazarus
   B. the crucifixion of Christ
   C. the creation of Adam
   D. the banishment of Adam from the Garden

15. **One method of testimony used in the novel is**
   A. letter-writing
   B. statistical data
   C. prayer
   D. speaking in tongues

16. **The self-aware and reflective nature of the novel largely stems from the fact that it is**
   A. retrospective
   B. cryptic
   C. apocalyptic
   D. salutary

17. **Frankenstein says that he chooses to recount his childhood in order to**
   A. give Walton his pedigree
   B. ensure that he will be remembered as a good person
   C. buy time while waiting for the monster
   D. account for the origins of the passion that led to his creating a monster

18. **According to Frankenstein, Newton's pursuit of scientific knowledge supposedly make him feel**
   A. like a god
   B. like a child
   C. like a hurricane
   D. like Socrates

19. **The monster's grotesqueness is ironic because**
   A. people besides Frankenstein thought the monster was beautiful
   B. Frankenstein aimed to create something beautiful
   C. the monster thought himself to be beautiful
   D. an earlier version of the monster was extremely beautiful

20. **The monster is most likely eloquent because**
   A. he was raised by a philosopher
   B. God was speaking through him
   C. he learned to speak from Paradise Lost
   D. Frankenstein is misremembering what he said

21. **William's death is ironic because**
   A. It is in no way ironic.
   B. he was killed by the result of an experiment to create life
   C. a prophecy said that he would not die for years hence
   D. his sister was born on the same day

22. **One insight offered by Frankenstein's experiment is that**
   A. the scope of science is limited
   B. scientific progress is always a positive enterprise
   C. all life is artificial
   D. scientific progress may sometimes be detrimental

23. **Frankenstein's description of scenery often reflects**
        A. lack of knowledge about the places he describes
        B. the expectations of Walton
        C. his mental state at the relevant time
        D. disinterest in what Walton takes from his story

24. **An example of how Frankenstein focalizes the passage of time is by describing a portrait of his**
        A. mother
        B. brother
        C. sister
        D. father

25. **One way in which Frankenstein presents the intensity of emotions is by**
        A. describing their bodily manifestations
        B. physically grabbing Walton at intense moments in his story
        C. omitting all emotional language
        D. often lapsing into stream-of-consciousness narration

Quiz 3 Answer Key

1. **(B)** natural law
2. **(B)** he believes that destiny binds him to his monster
3. **(A)** virtually the opposite of
4. **(A)** his father
5. **(C)** destiny
6. **(B)** providing his audience with verification of his story
7. **(C)** narrative unreliability
8. **(C)** moralizing
9. **(C)** smiled
10. **(A)** books
11. **(B)** justice
12. **(D)** stole fire from the gods
13. **(A)** references to poetry
14. **(C)** the creation of Adam
15. **(A)** letter-writing
16. **(A)** retrospective
17. **(D)** account for the origins of the passion that led to his creating a monster
18. **(B)** like a child
19. **(B)** Frankenstein aimed to create something beautiful
20. **(C)** he learned to speak from Paradise Lost
21. **(B)** he was killed by the result of an experiment to create life
22. **(D)** scientific progress may sometimes be detrimental
23. **(C)** his mental state at the relevant time
24. **(A)** mother
25. **(A)** describing their bodily manifestations

Frankenstein Quizzes

1. **Frankenstein often describes nature as**
   A. sexually arousing
   B. ultimately man-made
   C. sublime
   D. irrelevant

2. **Frankenstein often applies _____ to nature**
   A. personification
   B. statistical analysis
   C. sonnet composition
   D. anachronism

3. **A film version of Frankenstein was released in**
   A. 1995
   B. 1993
   C. 1994
   D. 1990

4. **Frankenstein built his monster out of**
   A. compost
   B. dead body parts
   C. a newborn baby
   D. scrap metal

5. **One thing that the monster learned from books was:**
   A. how to sing
   B. how to find Frankenstein
   C. how to feel new emotions
   D. how to smell accurately

6. **Both the monster and the novel are in part constituted by**
   A. dream theory
   B. ink
   C. older literary works
   D. the musings of a biomechanical engineer

7. **The major reason why Frankenstein's invention cannot truly be counted as 'progress' is because**
   A. False -- it is clearly progressive
   B. it yielded wholly negative consequences
   C. his work is disproven almost immediately
   D. he did not document his methods

8. **One could say that the novel makes the following thesis about science:**
      A. all potential scientific advancements are progressive of necessity
      B. all types are advancements are inherently progressive
      C. not all potential scientific advancements are progressive of necessity
      D. The novel makes no thesis about science.

9. **Frankenstein can be seen as a modern day retelling of**
      A. the Prometheus myth
      B. the Oedipus myth
      C. the Iliad
      D. the epic of Gilgamesh

10. **Central to Frankenstein's struggle is the question of**
      A. personal culpability for a creation's aspect
      B. whether or not one belongs to God
      C. whether Walton will absolve him of his sins
      D. whether the monster will learn to build a mate for himself

11. **The multiple forms of testimony and narrative within the text:**
      A. serves no substantial literary purpose
      B. adds to parallelism between text and monster
      C. ultimately implies that all testimony is a type of monologue
      D. is out-of-place in this type of story

12. **The scientific methodology behind the design of the monster suggests that the monster lacks**
      A. beauty
      B. logic
      C. free will
      D. power

13. **Frankenstein's family is**
      A. Swiss
      B. English
      C. Russian
      D. South African

14. **When Caroline Frankenstein found Elizabeth, the girl was living**
      A. alone
      B. at university
      C. with a wealthy benefactor
      D. with a penniless Italian family

15. **Frankenstein's first object of true worship was:**
    A. Elizabeth
    B. alchemy
    C. his father
    D. his monster

16. **A major element of Frankenstein's storytelling is**
    A. foreshadowing
    B. encoded messages
    C. musical allusions
    D. guessing what the monster would think of his childhood

17. **Clerval cannot follow Frankenstein to university initially because**
    A. Clerval's father forbids it
    B. Clerval is not smart enough
    C. Clerval is too young
    D. Clerval is ill at the time

18. **The first person whom Frankenstein encounters at Ingolstadt is**
    A. Krempe
    B. his father
    C. Frankenstein never travels to Ingolstadt
    D. the monster

19. **Frankenstein's research leading up to his creation of the monster includes**
    A. traveling to America for inspiration
    B. meditating for days on end
    C. torturing living creatures
    D. discussing the matter at length with his father

20. **Frankenstein learns of the death of William from**
    A. a message from Clerval
    B. the monster, who gloats about it
    C. a letter from Elizabeth
    D. a letter from his father

21. **When Frankenstein returns to Geneva, a flash of lightning illuminates**
    A. the steeple of a church
    B. Clerval's vacant face
    C. the monster
    D. a field of slaughtered oxen

22. **Frankenstein decides against confessing to William's murder because**
        A. he knows his confession will be discredited because he was in Ingoldstadt at the time
        B. he is afraid of the consequences
        C. He never considers confessing.
        D. the monster threatens him

23. **When Justine is tried for William's murder, _____ speaks on her behalf.**
        A. a group of townspeople
        B. no one
        C. Frankestein
        D. Eliabeth

24. **Frankenstein loses faith in humanity's essential goodness following**
        A. the execution of Justine
        B. the death of William
        C. the death of Frankenstein's father
        D. the first appearance of the monster

25. **The monster's first memories are of**
        A. the words of his creator
        B. the past lives of the dead people of which he is composed
        C. a barrage of sensory perceptions
        D. killing William

Quiz 4 Answer Key

1. **(C)** sublime
2. **(A)** personification
3. **(C)** 1994
4. **(B)** dead body parts
5. **(C)** how to feel new emotions
6. **(C)** older literary works
7. **(B)** it yielded wholly negative consequences
8. **(C)** not all potential scientific advancements are progressive of necessity
9. **(A)** the Prometheus myth
10. **(A)** personal culpability for a creation's aspect
11. **(B)** adds to parallelism between text and monster
12. **(C)** free will
13. **(A)** Swiss
14. **(D)** with a penniless Italian family
15. **(A)** Elizabeth
16. **(A)** foreshadowing
17. **(A)** Clerval's father forbids it
18. **(A)** Krempe
19. **(C)** torturing living creatures
20. **(D)** a letter from his father
21. **(C)** the monster
22. **(A)** he knows his confession will be discredited because he was in Ingoldstadt at the time
23. **(D)** Eliabeth
24. **(A)** the execution of Justine
25. **(C)** a barrage of sensory perceptions

Frankenstein Bibliography

Jessica Montalvo, author of ClassicNote. Completed on February 25, 2000, copyright held by GradeSaver.

Updated and revised by Aaron Suduiko June 12, 2015. Copyright held by GradeSaver.

Shelley, Mary. Frankenstein. London: Henry Colburn and Richard Bentley, 1831.

Mary Shelley; J. Paul Hunter, Ed.. Frankenstein, Second Norton Critical Edition. New York: W. W. Norton & Company, 2012.

"Frankenstein." Literature.org. June 4, 2015. <http://literature.org/authors/ shelley-mary/frankenstein/>.

William Smith, Ed.. "A Dictionary of Greek and Roman biography and mythology: Prometheus.." Perseus Digital Library. 1873. June 4, 2015. <http://www.perseus.tufts.edu/hopper/ text?doc=Perseus%3Atext%3A1999.04.0104%3Aalphabetic+letter%3DP%3Aentr bio-1>.

"Mary Shelley's Frankenstein." IMDb. June 4, 2015. <http://www.imdb.com/title/tt0109836/>.

Peter Menzies. "Counterfactual Theories of Causation." Stanford Encyclopedia of Philosophy. February 10, 2014. June 4, 2015. <http://plato.stanford.edu/entries/causation-counterfactual/>.

Essay Dr. Jekyll and Mr. Frankenstein

by Theoderek Wayne

Both Robert Louis Stevenson's Dr. Jekyll and Mr. Hyde and Mary Shelley's Frankenstein tell cautionary tales of scientists abusing their creative powers to exist in another sphere where they cannot be directly blamed for their actions. Though Frankenstein's creation is a "Creature" distinct from his creator while Dr. Jekyll metamorphoses into Mr. Hyde, the "double" of each protagonist progressively grows more violent throughout his story. By doing so he symbolizes his creator's repressed desires in a stifling society.

The stories have parallel structures in the three main ways. First, both Dr. Jekyll and Frankenstein are scientists who, though welcomed by society, find it constraining and often alienate themselves. Each creates an alter ego for himself to live out his liberated passions, Hyde for Jekyll and the Creature for Frankenstein. Jekyll creates his with intention for evil and Frankenstein with the idea of building a supreme being. However, it could be argued that Frankenstein unconsciously wishes his creation to commit acts of sin. Hyde's and Frankenstein's first victims are children. They each evolve over time and develop their violent tendencies, culminating in the murder of a well-esteemed man for Hyde and Frankenstein's family and friends.

The first mention of Dr. Jekyll comes in a discussion between his longtime friends, Lanyon and Utterson, men whose names imply a traditional, hampered society. "Utterson" combines both "utter," connoting a squelched speech, with "son," defining the society's patriarchal structure, and "Lanyon" casts images of sprawling canyons that are noticeably absent in the gray, foggy London Stevenson depicts. Lanyon admits he sees little of Jekyll anymore; according to Lanyon, "'He began to go wrong, wrong in mind; and though of course I continue to take an interest in him for old sake's sake, as they say, I see and have seen devilish little of the man'" (12). Jekyll's associations with demonic and insane imagery contrasts with the well-polished society from which he struggles to extricate himself. His self-imposed isolation is the least harmful manner he uses to show his displeasure with society.

Frankenstein similarly isolates himself. Under the guise of protecting his friends and fiancée from the Creature that stalks him, the scientist decides to leave England instead of marrying: "My journey had been my own suggestion, and Elizabeth, therefore, acquiesced; but she was filled with disquiet at the idea of my suffering, away from her, the inroads of misery and grief" (149). However, Frankenstein cannot muster the same emotion: "I remembered only, and it was with a bitter anguish that I reflected on it, to order that my chemical instruments should be packed to go with me" (149). Frankenstein also has a penchant for working alone; like Dr. Jekyll, he is emotionally detached from a society that expects him to fulfill various obligations, and he accordingly responds with physical detachment.

Both Hyde and the Creature choose children for their first victims. According to an eyewitness, Hyde "trampled calmly over the child's body and left her screaming on the ground...He was perfectly cool and made no resistance, but gave me one look, so ugly that it brought out the sweat on me like running" (4-5). Hyde is a deformed character who evokes horror and disgust in those who contact him. He lashes out in this seemingly chance encounter, but his trampling a child's body, a figure of innocence that would find his scarred visage doubly repugnant, is indicative of his deep-rooted discontentment with his environment and his own psyche. The reaction he provokes from the crowd confirms his masochistic tendencies. As an eyewitness reports, "I never saw a circle of such hateful faces; and there was the man in the middle, with a kind of black, sneering coolness-frightened too, I could see that-but carrying it off, sir, really like Satan" (5). The very name "Hyde" serves a double meaning: both a haven, a "hyde" where the upstanding Jekyll can sequester himself, and an animal's skin. Hyde is incredibly animalistic; simian elements are conjured up when he is described in a later confrontation: "Hyde broke out of all bounds and clubbed him to the earth. And next moment, with ape-like fury, he was trampling his victim under foot and hailing down a storm of blows" (27). Words like "bounds," "clubbed," "earth," "ape-like," and "storm" all reinforce the reader's idea of Hyde being a thoroughly primitive savage, and the repetition of "trampling" serves as an excellent mini-motif. Though Hyde tramples his victims, has he not been trampled in the same way by the oppressive society that condemns him at a glance?

The Creature murders Frankenstein's younger brother, but he, too, is driven to that course of action by a society that scorns him. The Creature spies on a family in the wilderness and learns human language, customs, and history. He resembles nothing so much as a child or prehistoric man in these episodes, first discovering fire, then bits of language, and finally emotion. He confronts the elderly father of the family and predicts his fate if he is not taken in by them: "I am full of fears, for if I fail there, I am an outcast in the world forever" (129). Fulfilling his prophesy, the rest of the family barges in: "Who can describe their horror and consternation upon beholding me?" (131) The Creature's status as pariah differs in one major respect from Hyde's; though they both possess loathsome appearances, the Creature's soul, at the beginning of his life, at least, is as pure as could be hoped for, while Hyde's black heart shows in his face.

Both Hyde and Creature turn more vicious and more reactive to society. Hyde's second incident is the murder of an "aged beautiful gentleman with white hair," precisely what he can never hope to be (26). Hyde uses a stick to club his victim to death: "The stick with which the deed had been done, although it was of some rare and very tough and heavy wood, had broken in the middle under the stress of this insensate cruelty; and one splintered half had rolled in the neighbouring gutter-the other, without doubt, had been carried away by the murderer" (28). The broken stick, a gift from Utterson to Jekyll, further emphasizes the duality of man's nature, and half of its destination, the gutter, outlines Stevenson's view of that nature. As Jekyll confesses, "I was the first that could plod in the public eye with a load of genial respectability, and in a moment, like a schoolboy, strip off these lendings and spring headlong into the sea of liberty. But for me, in my impenetrable mantle, the safety was complete. Think of it-I did not even exist!" (86) Hyde has fully broken through and exhausted his rage on the society of Sir Danvers Carew; he has evolved from a forum for "naughty pleasures" to a minor terrorist of children to a full-fledged murderer. He acts out Jekyll's own dark nature, perverting the stick, a gift that once symbolized a societal bond, into a weapon that tears apart its environment.

The Creature continues a string of murders of Frankenstein's family. Frankenstein's reaction to the murder of his friend Clerval reveals that he, too, perhaps had this evil side that he could not act upon: "'Have my murderous machinations deprived you also, my dearest Henry, of life? Two I have already destroyed; other victims await their destiny: but you, Clerval, my friend, my benefactor-'" (171) Though this speech could be read as Frankenstein's first assumption of guilt, indirect as it may be, one could also analyze it as an admission that he has been behind every murder from the inception. He is not as aware as Jekyll is of his own lust for evil, but his monstrous side shows up in his isolationist dealings and his God-complex that reveals his desire for a new society.

Hyde and the Creature's plights follow similar paths, but their motives seem somewhat different. Jekyll invented Hyde for a dive in which he could transport himself and put on display his evil psyche. Frankenstein assembled the Creature as an über-man of sorts, a prototype of a better society. Frankenstein was published in 1818, Dr. Jekyll and Mr. Hyde in 1886. Perhaps Stevenson's book marks the end of Romanticism as a viable literary style in modern times. Though Frankenstein's evil hides is veiled by guilt and a seemingly upstanding society position, Jekyll's is visibly apparent. Frankenstein is a shaded man with no clear dividing line, whereas Jekyll is a black-and-white character with a subset of colors inside his dichotomies. Stevenson, drawing on Shelley's story, reflected both a new literary movement and a new psychological study.

Essay Egotism, Personal Glory, and the Pursuit for Immortality

by Tiffany Guinan

The desire to make history to discover what remains undiscovered, or to know what remains unknown is a timeless human goal. Although many have failed to realize this dream, a very few have been wildly successful in its pursuit. The immortality afforded these select few has, of course, only served to encourage those who come after. Mary Wollstonecraft Shelley's Frankenstein is a literary meditation upon this intensely human desire here exemplified by the title character's quest for personal glory by means of scientific discovery.

Both Victor Frankenstein and the Arctic explorer Robert Walton, whose letters open the novel, possess an insatiable thirst for privileged knowledge of those things that are unknown to the common man. Shelley presents their stories as being in some sense parallel to each other: each is a failure, and each suffers from the same fatal flaw. Walton, a voyager, explores the secrets of the natural earth, in the company of a crew of men on the same mission. Victor works in solitude to penetrate secrets of a metaphysical nature: namely, the principle of life. Though they explore entirely different realms, Walton and Victor are both bound by a common cause. Each longs to further the knowledge of mankind and to glorify his own name.

The reader is invited to stand in the place of Mrs. Seville, Walton's sister and the recipient of his letters. The selfishness of Walton's ambition is not immediately apparent; it only becomes clear when the reader takes the subtleties of Walton's point of view into account (Walling 35). In his opening letter, Walton attempts to assure his sister that he is safe and to remind her of the reason for his journey: he wishes to confer an "inestimable benefit"(2) upon all mankind. The reader may initially perceive this wish as sincere, but this is not precisely the case. Above all else, Walton craves fame, and he presents his desire as altruistic only in order to inspire his beloved sister's admiration. She, for her part, had anticipated his journey with "evil forebodings" (1).

In his ensuing letters he speaks of his intrepid crew, first briefly introducing his lieutenant, whom he describes as "madly desirous of glory"(5). It is clear that Walton assumes that his crew has the same passion for this journey that he does; he believes that they would willingly sacrifice their lives for the cause. Walton's assumption is spectacularly mistaken, and reveals him as utterly insensitive to the real motivations of his crew. Walton goes on to say that the life of one man would be "a small price to pay" (11) for the success of the expedition and the advancement of the entire race.

Walton's "cause," however, is nothing more than his lust for fame hardly edifying to humanity as a whole. Walton's self-regard becomes apparent in that he never once asks about his sister's well being, despite the fact that he has not seen her for a number of years. He believes that she is pining for him and spends every moment awaiting his return. In each of the letters, Walton reveals the disproportionate quality of his ambition through his redundant references to "glory", "admiration" and "triumph."

Victor Frankenstein desires to acquire knowledge hidden from the eyes of the common man. He talks of ridding the world of disease as a means of making man immortal. Although his altruism seems genuine, the personal glory that his discovery would provide him dominates his thoughts. He aspires to the absolute, unlimited powers of a god, and believes himself to be a genius, with a natural propensity to discover the secret of life itself. He declares to Walton that men of his extraordinary intelligence "however erroneously directed" (28) almost always provide new benefits for mankind.

The danger of pride and egotism is one of the novel's central themes (Kiely 166). Significantly, Victor begins his tale with the story of Beaufort, a man whose pride results in his own demise, thereby leaving his daughter an orphan. It is from the union of this girl with the elder Frankenstein that Victor is born.

The decision to adopt Elizabeth Lavenza ends Victor's days as an only child. If the dangers of pride and egotism are a part of the novel's foundation, then the horrors of isolation serve as one of its beams of support. Shelley seems to suggest that solitude gives rise to pride and self-love; intimate companionship is thus an absolute necessity for living a moral life.

It is significant that, in Victor's mind, Elizabeth does not join the family as an equal member but as a "gift" to him; it is as though his parents recognized the hazards presented by his solitude and attempted to save him from them. Even after Elizabeth joins the family and a second child is subsequently born, Victor elects to be alone, avoiding crowds and having only a single close friend. He seems almost proud of his introversion: he regards it as an emblem of his individuality, his elevation above the common man.

The novel reflects Wollstonecraft Shelley's own philosophical views. She alludes to Jean-Jacques Rousseau, a philosopher of the French Enlightenment, whose theories greatly interested her. Rousseau argued that humanity was in essence good; only the influence of society led to the corruption of man. He also argued, somewhat contradictorily, that humans are at birth weak and innocent and thus require guidance and proper education. Without such guidance, the nature of the isolated man would become irretrievably degraded by society. Rousseau maintained that "A man left entirely to himself from birth would be the most misshapen of creatures" (Stevenson 110). This notion is absolutely crucial to Frankenstein: while it undoubtedly applies to Victor, it finds its most direct and literal illustration in the character of the monster.

Frankenstein's research, as well as the desire for fame that animates it, so entrances him that he neglects his family and friends. He works in solitude; thus isolated, he becomes incapable of resisting his obsession. The obsessional quality of his labors is apparent in his description of himself through such words as "unremitting", "dedicated", "tortured", "resistless", "frantic", and "engaged" (33). He admits that he had become "pale with study", "emaciated with confinement"; he was so focused on his endeavors that he "lost all soul or sensation but for this one pursuit" (34).

<I>Frankenstein</i> was written during the period of the first industrial

revolution, and it contributed to some of the developing ideas of the age. The novel (like the Marxist theory that it might be said to prefigure) implies that men embody themselves through their creations (Wolff 153). Wollstonecraft Shelley extends this idea to suggest that a creation can only be a magnified image of its creator.

Many critics have argued that <I>Frankenstein</I> lacks complex characterization, insofar as Victor and his monster have the same personality. The confusion of the name of the creator with that of his monster (who is deliberately given no name) is but one example of the results of this misreading. These critics fail to recognize the philosophical implications inherent in Victor's mirroring of his monster and vice versa. As man was made in the image of god, the creature is made in the image of his creator Frankenstein. The novel makes this connection explicit through the monster's realization that his form is but a "filthy type" of Frankenstein's own (93).

It is on a "dreary night of November"(34) that Frankenstein finally realizes his ambition; the concrete accomplishment, however, spectacularly fails to approximate the ideal (Kiely 162). Victor's creature-child (the prodigious birth of his unholy experiment) is cobbled together out of fragments of the dead; though Victor chose the fragments for their beauty, the monster is grotesquely ugly. Victor describes the creature as a "catastrophe", a "wretch" and finally, a "monster" (35); this rapid progression indicates the speed with which his hope of immortality has led instead to ruin. Frankenstein's decision to abandon his creature reveals his "scientific" pretensions to be a sham: he flees, rather than examining the creature to determine the reason for his failure (Kiely 172).

In creating the monster, Victor longed to produce a superior race of men. The monster can be seen as Victor's "child": he is a reproduction of Victor (his uncanny double). The creature, like a child, is expected to mirror Frankenstein's own desires; Frankenstein imagines that this "new human" will be infinitely grateful to him, and will overwhelm his creator with worship (Brooks 224). The relationship between creator and creation reproduces the Biblical myth of the creation of man albeit in a non-Christian context (Levine 11). Although Victor wishes to play the role of god, he lacks the requisite knowledge (recall that the Christian god is held to be omniscient). His human imperfections can only conceive of something less than himself. The monster thus becomes an eternal self-inflicted wound upon his creator, and serves as a horrific embodiment of the consequences of hubris and ambition.

Appropriately enough, Victor Frankenstein begins his cautionary tale with a warning against the overzealous pursuit of knowledge: "How much happier that man is who believes his native town to be the world, than he who aspires to become greater than his nature will allow" (31). His reference to knowledge as a "serpent"(13) once again recalls the Christian myth of Creation: Adam and Eve were cast out of Paradise because a <I>serpent</I> persuaded them to eat of the Tree of <I>Knowledge</I>. Frankenstein's tale has a profound effect upon Walton: he is filled with remorse for endangering the lives of his crew, and thus consents to turn the ship about. His "moral transformation" is hardly complete, however: he is furious at being deprived of his chance at glory. Frankenstein, too, is hardly redeemed by book's end: he raises himself from his deathbed to exhort Walton's crew to continue their expedition despite the fact that they will thus be courting death. He instructs them to "be men" and to be dauntless in the face of the "danger and death" that surround them; only in this way, he maintains, can they acquire glory and avoid disgrace.

Victor Frankenstein dies a failure, insistent that his fate is an "accident of circumstance, the result of insufficient knowledge, or an imperfection in nature itself" (Kiely 160). Though he tells Walton to "avoid ambition" (162), he blames nature itself for his failure and fails to take responsibility for the catastrophic effects of his selfish pursuits. In the world of Mary Shelley's <I>Frankenstein</I>, redemption (at least for mere men) remains impossible.

Bibliography

Brooks, Peter. "'Godlike Science/ Unhallowed Arts': Language, Nature,and Monstrosity". The Endurance of Frankenstein. Ed. George Levine. Berkeley: University of California Press, 1979.

Kiely, Robert. The Romantic Novel in England. Cambridge: Harvard University Press, 1972.

Levine, George. "The Ambiguous Heritage of Frankenstein". The Endurance of Frankenstein. Ed. George Levine. Berkeley: University of California Press, 1979. 3-30.

Shelley, Mary. Frankenstein. Ed. Candace Ward. New York, Dover, 1994. Based on a reproduction of the third edition of 1831, as originally published by Colburn and Bentley (London).

Spark, Muriel. Mary Shelley. New York: E.P. Dutton, 1987.

Stevenson, Leslie. The Study of Human Nature: A Reader. New York: Oxford University Press, 2000.

Walling, William A. Mary Shelley. New York: Twayne, 1972.

Wolff, Robert P. About Philosophy. Upper Saddle River, NJ: Prentice Hall, 1998.

ClassicNotes

GradeSaver™

Getting you the grade since 1999™

Other ClassicNotes from GradeSaver™

Aristotle: Nicomachean Ethics
Aristotle's Poetics
Aristotle's Politics
Arms and the Man
A Room of One's Own
A Room With a View
A Rose For Emily and Other Short Stories
Around the World in 80 Days
A Separate Peace
As I Lay Dying
A Streetcar Named Desire
Astrophil and Stella
A Study in Scarlet
As You Like It
A Tale of Two Cities

A Thousand Splendid Suns
Atlas Shrugged
Atonement
A Very Old Man With Enormous Wings
A Vindication of the Rights of Woman
A White Heron and Other Stories
A Wrinkle in Time
Babbitt
Balzac and the Little Chinese Seamstress
Bartleby the Scrivener
Bastard Out of Carolina
Beloved
Benito Cereno
Beowulf

Bhagavad-Gita
Billy Budd
Black Beauty
Black Boy
Blade Runner
Bleak House
Bless Me, Ultima
Blindness
Blood Meridian: Or the Evening Redness in the West
Blood Wedding
Bluest Eye
Brave New World
Breakfast at Tiffany's
Breakfast of Champions
Burmese Days
By Night in Chile
Call of the Wild
Candide

For our full list of over 250 Study Guides, Quizzes,
Sample College Application Essays, Literature Essays and E-texts, visit:

www.gradesaver.com

ClassicNotes

GradeSaver™

Getting you the grade since 1999™

Other ClassicNotes from GradeSaver™

Cannery Row
Casablanca
Catch-22
Catching Fire
Cathedral
Cat on a Hot Tin
  Roof
Cat's Cradle
Charlie and the
  Chocolate Factory
Charlotte's Web
Charlotte Temple
Chinese Cinderella
Christina Rossetti:
  Poems
Christopher
  Marlowe's Poems
Chronicle of a Death
  Foretold
Citizen Kane
Civil Disobedience
Civilization and Its
  Discontents

Civil Peace
Cloud Atlas
Coleridge's Poems
Comedy of Errors
Communist
  Manifesto
Confessions
Confessions of an
  English Opium
  Eater
Connecticut Yankee
  in King Arthur's
  Court
Coriolanus
Crewel
Crime and
  Punishment
Cry, the Beloved
  Country
Cymbeline
Cyrano de Bergerac
Daisy Miller
David Copperfield

Death and the King's
  Horseman
Death and the
  Maiden
Death in Venice
Death of a Salesman
Democracy in
  America
Desire Under the
  Elms
Devil in a Blue
  Dress
Dharma Bums
Disgrace
Divergent
Divine Comedy-I:
  Inferno
Do Androids Dream
  of Electric Sheep?
Doctor Faustus
  (Marlowe)
Don Quixote Book I

For our full list of over 250 Study Guides, Quizzes,
Sample College Application Essays, Literature Essays and E-texts, visit:

www.gradesaver.com

ClassicNotes

GradeSaver™

Getting you the grade since 1999™

Other ClassicNotes from GradeSaver™

Don Quixote Book II

Dora: An Analysis of a Case of Hysteria

Dracula

Dr. Jekyll and Mr. Hyde

Dubliners

East of Eden

Edgar Huntly: Memoirs of a Sleep-Walker

Educating Rita

Electra by Sophocles

Emily Dickinson's Collected Poems

Emma

Ender's Game

Endgame

Enduring Love

Enrique's Journey

Equus

Esperanza Rising

Eternal Sunshine of the Spotless Mind

Ethan Frome

Eugene Onegin

Evelina

Everyday Use

Everyman: Morality Play

Everything is Illuminated

Exeter Book

Extremely Loud and Incredibly Close

Ezra Pound: Poems

Fahrenheit 451

Fallen Angels

Fear and Loathing in Las Vegas

Fences

Fifth Business

Fight Club

Fight Club (Film)

Flags of Our Fathers

Flannery O'Connor's Stories

Flight

For Colored Girls Who Have Considered Suicide When the Rainbow Is Enuf

For Whom the Bell Tolls

Founding Brothers

Frankenstein

Franny and Zooey

Friday Night Lights

Fun Home

Gargantua and Pantagruel

Goethe's Faust

Gorilla, My Love

Great Expectations

Grendel

For our full list of over 250 Study Guides, Quizzes,
Sample College Application Essays, Literature Essays and E-texts, visit:

www.gradesaver.com

ClassicNotes

GradeSaver™

Getting you the grade since 1999™

Other ClassicNotes from GradeSaver™

Keats' Poems and
  Letters
Kidnapped
King Lear
King Solomon's
  Mines
Kokoro
Kurt Vonnegut's
  Short Stories
Lady Chatterley's
  Lover
Lancelot: Or, the
  Knight of the Cart
Langston Hughes:
  Poems
Last of the
  Mohicans
Leaves of Grass
Left to Tell
Legend
Le Morte d'Arthur
Les Miserables

Letter From
  Birmingham Jail
Leviathan
Libation Bearers
Life is Beautiful
Life of Pi
Light In August
Like Water for
  Chocolate
Little Women
Lolita
Long Day's Journey
  Into Night
Look Back in Anger
Looking for Alaska
Lord Byron's Poems
Lord Jim
Lord of the Flies
Love in the Time of
  Cholera
Love Medicine
Lucy
Lying Awake

Macbeth
Madame Bovary
Maestro
Maggie: A Girl of
  the Streets and
  Other Stories
Manhattan Transfer
Mankind: Medieval
  Morality Plays
Mansfield Park
Mary Barton
Master Harold...
  And the Boys
Matched
Matthew Arnold:
  Poems
MAUS
Measure for
  Measure
Medea
Merchant of Venice
Metamorphoses
Midaq Alley

For our full list of over 250 Study Guides, Quizzes,
Sample College Application Essays, Literature Essays and E-texts, visit:

www.gradesaver.com

ClassicNotes

GradeSaver™

Getting you the grade since 1999™

ClassicNotes

GradeSaver™

Getting you the grade since 1999™

Other ClassicNotes from GradeSaver™

Short Stories of Ernest Hemingway

Short Stories of F. Scott Fitzgerald

Siddhartha

Silas Marner

Silence

Sir Gawain and the Green Knight

Sir Thomas Wyatt: Poems

Sister Carrie

Six Characters in Search of an Author

Slaughterhouse Five

Snow Country

Snow Falling on Cedars

Something Wicked This Way Comes

Song of Roland

Song of Solomon

Songs of Innocence and of Experience

Sonny's Blues

Sons and Lovers

Speak

Spenser's Amoretti and Epithalamion

Spring Awakening

Sula

Sundiata: An Epic of Old Mali

Sylvia Plath: Poems

Symposium by Plato

Tartuffe

Tell Me a Riddle

Tender is the Night

Tennyson's Poems

Tess of the D'Urbervilles

The Absolutely True Diary of a Part-Time Indian

The Adventures of Augie March

The Adventures of Huckleberry Finn

The Adventures of Tom Sawyer

The Aeneid

The Age of Innocence

The Alchemist (Coelho)

The Alchemist (Jonson)

The Ambassadors

The Analects of Confucius

The Arabian Nights: One Thousand and One Nights

The Autobiography of an Ex-Colored Man

The Awakening

For our full list of over 250 Study Guides, Quizzes,
Sample College Application Essays, Literature Essays and E-texts, visit:

www.gradesaver.com

ClassicNotes

Gr**A**deSaver™

Getting you the grade since 1999™

Other ClassicNotes from GradeSaver™

The Bacchae

The Bean Trees

The Beggar's Opera

The Bell Jar

The Birthday Party

The Blithedale
Romance

The Bloody
Chamber

The Bonfire of the
Vanities

The Book of Daniel

The Book of the
Duchess and
Other Poems

The Book Thief

The Boy in the
Striped Pajamas

The Brief Wondrous
Life of Oscar Wao

The Brothers
Karamazov

The Burning Plain
and Other Stories

The Canterbury
Tales

The Caretaker

The Catcher in the
Rye

The Caucasian
Chalk Circle

The Cherry Orchard

The Chocolate War

The Chosen

The
Chrysanthemums

The Circle

The Collector

The Color of Water

The Color Purple

The Consolation of
Philosophy

The Coquette

The Count of Monte
Cristo

The Country of the
Pointed Firs and
Other Stories

The Country Wife

The Cricket in
Times Square

The Crucible

The Crying of Lot
49

The Curious
Incident of the
Dog in the Night-
time

The Death of Ivan
Ilych

The Devil and Tom
Walker

The Devil's
Arithmetic

The Diary of a
Young Girl by
Anne Frank

For our full list of over 250 Study Guides, Quizzes,
Sample College Application Essays, Literature Essays and E-texts, visit:

www.gradesaver.com

ClassicNotes

GradeSaver™

Getting you the grade since 1999™

Other ClassicNotes from GradeSaver™

The Jew of Malta

The Joy Luck Club

The Jungle

The Kite Runner

The Lais of Marie
de France

The Legend of
Sleepy Hollow

The Life of Olaudah
Equiano

The Lion, the Witch
and the Wardrobe

The Lone Ranger
and Tonto
Fistfight in
Heaven

The Lord of the
Rings: The
Fellowship of the
Ring

The Lord of the
Rings: The Return
of the King

The Lord of the
Rings: The Two
Towers

The Lottery and
Other Stories

The Lovely Bones

The Love Song of J.
Alfred Prufrock

The Man of Mode

The Marrow of
Tradition

The Master and
Margarita

The Mayor of
Casterbridge

The Maze Runner

The Metamorphosis

The Mill on the
Floss

The Monk

The Moonstone

The Most
Dangerous Game

The Murder of
Roger Ackroyd

The Namesake

The Narrative of
Arthur Gordon
Pym of Nantucket

The Odyssey

The Old Man and
the Sea

The Origin of
Species

The Outsiders

The Pearl

The Perks of Being
a Wallflower

The Piano Lesson

The Picture of
Dorian Gray

The Playboy of the
Western World

The Poems of
William Blake

For our full list of over 250 Study Guides, Quizzes,
Sample College Application Essays, Literature Essays and E-texts, visit:

www.gradesaver.com

ClassicNotes

GradeSaver™

Getting you the grade since 1999™

Other ClassicNotes from GradeSaver™

The Poisonwood Bible

The Portrait of a Lady

The Praise of Folly

The Prince

The Professor's House

The Quiet American

The Ramayana

The Real Inspector Hound

The Real Life of Sebastian Knight

The Red Badge of Courage

The Remains of the Day

The Republic

Therese Raquin

The Revenger's Tragedy

The Rime of the Ancient Mariner

The Road

The Rover

The Sandman

The Satanic Verses

The Scarlet Ibis

The Scarlet Letter

The Scarlet Pimpernel

The Seagull

The Secret Life of Bees

The Secret River

The Social Contract

The Sorrows of Young Werther

The Souls of Black Folk

The Sound and the Fury

The Sound of Waves

The Sovereignty and Goodness of God

The Spanish Tragedy

The Spirit Catches You and You Fall Down

The Stranger

The Sun Also Rises

The Taming of the Shrew

The Tempest

The Testing

The Theory of Moral Sentiments

The Things They Carried

The Threepenny Opera

The Time Machine

The Tortilla Curtain

The Trials of Brother Jero

For our full list of over 250 Study Guides, Quizzes,
Sample College Application Essays, Literature Essays and E-texts, visit:

www.gradesaver.com

Made in the USA
Coppell, TX
23 May 2020